Day by Day with God

Edited by Jackie Harris   September–December 2023

Writers in this issue

Chris Leonard is an author and leads writing groups and creative writing holidays. She is a grandmother and has also become an 'Anna Friend' and enjoys leading memory groups for the elderly. Find out more at **chrisleonardwriting.uk**.

Tanya Marlow is a lecturer in pastoral theology and a popular speaker and writer. She specialises in *narratio divina* (storytelling in biblical studies) and theologies of disability and suffering. Find her at **tanyamarlow.com**.

Michele D. Morrison is a freelance writer, wife, mother and grandmother. She loves digging into God's word, listening for God's voice in the daily routines of life and blogging at **tearsamidthealiencorn.blogspot.com**.

Sheila Jacobs is a writer, an editor and an award-winning author. She lives in rural north Essex, attends an Elim church where she serves as deacon and is a day chaplain at a retreat centre.

Sandra Wheatley lives in Newcastle and loves to share God's encouragements through her writing and extensive prayer ministry. Due to the rapid onset of MS, retirement came early from her nursing career.

Amy Boucher Pye is a writer, speaker, retreat leader and spiritual director. She's the author of several books, including the new *Holding Onto Hope* (BRF, 2023). Find her at **amyboucherpye.com**.

Mary Reid was the first editor of *Day by Day with God*. Since retiring from teaching and publishing work, she lives in Suffolk with her husband and enjoys being part of a lively church and community.

Elaine Storkey is an academic, author, broadcaster and senior member of Newnham College, Cambridge. A former president of Tearfund, she also directed the London Institute for Contemporary Christianity for ten years and has taught in universities both in the UK and overseas.

Plus, guest contributors **Sara Batts-Neale**, a priest in the diocese of Chelmsford; **Chine McDonald**, director of the Theos think tank; **Claire Musters**, writer and speaker; **Bridget Plass**, writer and speaker; and **Alianore Smith**, church partnership manager for International Justice Mission UK.

September–December 2023

Day by Day
with
God

Rooting women's lives in the Bible

BRF

15 The Chambers, Vineyard
Abingdon OX14 3FE
brf.org.uk

Bible Reading Fellowship is a charity (233280)
and company limited by guarantee (301324),
registered in England and Wales

ISBN 978 1 80039 182 6
All rights reserved

This edition © 2023 Bible Reading Fellowship
Cover image © Yakobchuk Olena/stock.adobe.com

Distributed in Australia by:
MediaCom Education Inc, PO Box 610, Unley, SA 5061
Tel: 1 800 811 311 | admin@mediacom.org.au

Distributed in New Zealand by:
Scripture Union Wholesale, PO Box 760, Wellington
Tel: 04 385 0421 | suwholesale@clear.net.nz

Acknowledgements
Scripture quotations marked with the following abbreviations are taken from the version
shown. Where no abbreviation is given, the quotation is taken from the same version
as the headline reference. MSG: *The Message*, copyright © 1993, 1994, 1995, 1996, 2000,
2001, 2002 by Eugene H. Peterson. Used by permission of NavPress. All rights reserved.
Represented by Tyndale House Publishers, Inc. NIV: The Holy Bible, New International
Version (Anglicised edition) copyright © 1979, 1984, 2011 by Biblica. Used by permission
of Hodder & Stoughton Publishers, a Hachette UK company. All rights reserved. 'NIV' is a
registered trademark of Biblica. UK trademark number 1448790. ESV: The Holy Bible, English
Standard Version, published by HarperCollins Publishers, © 2001 Crossway Bibles, a division
of Good News Publishers. Used by permission. All rights reserved. NRSV: The New Revised
Standard Version of the Bible, Anglicised edition, copyright © 1989, 1995 by the Division of
Christian Education of the National Council of the Churches of Christ in the United States of
America. Used by permission. All rights reserved. TPT: The Passion Translation®. Copyright
© 2017, 2018, 2020 by Passion & Fire Ministries, Inc. Used by permission. All rights reserved.
thePassionTranslation.com. NLT: The Holy Bible, New Living Translation, copyright © 1996,
2004, 2007, 2013. Used by permission of Tyndale House Publishers, Inc., Carol Stream,
Illinois 60188. All rights reserved. CEV: The Contemporary English Version. New Testament
© American Bible Society 1991, 1992, 1995. Old Testament © American Bible Society 1995.
Anglicisations © British & Foreign Bible Society 1996. Used by permission. TLB: The Living
Bible copyright © 1971 by Tyndale House Foundation. Used by permission of Tyndale House
Publishers Inc., Carol Stream, Illinois 60188. All rights reserved.

A catalogue record for this book is available from the British Library

Printed and bound by Gutenberg Press, Tarxien, Malta

Welcome

Thank you for joining us to study God's word. You're in the company of women who know the value of regular Bible reading. We live in challenging times, but we believe that as we engage with God's word we will find encouragement, strength and a new vision of what God wants to do both in us and through us.

In this issue, we welcome back Mary Reid, a previous editor of *Day by Day with God*, who takes us through Paul's second letter to the Thessalonians. It's a letter written to help Christians living in a complicated society, so it is very relevant for us today.

We also welcome Tanya Marlow to our team of contributors. Tanya is an author, speaker and broadcaster on faith and spirituality, as well as a campaigner for those with chronic illness. Through the lives of different women in the Bible, Tanya considers some of the challenges we face in our working lives. However, this isn't just about the paid work we do; we're encouraged to think about all the different roles we have, the things we do and how we do them.

Elsewhere, we draw practical advice for daily life from the book of Proverbs, learn how we can use scripture to help us conquer the 'giants' in our lives, find inspiration from Noah and survey David's prayer life. We'll also take some time to focus on God's kindness, to think about how we prepare for Christmas and then to reflect on the Christmas story and God's good news for all people.

We begin with a study on celebrations. In God's goodness, he designed times of rest, remembrance and celebration for his people. There was a rhythm to life that perhaps we need to rediscover, and it seems fitting to think about this as we approach the autumn and winter months with our own celebrations of Harvest, Remembrance, Advent and Christmas.

We're excited for the changes God is going to bring into our lives as we step aside from the noise and make time to listen to his word. May we know that whatever is happening around us, we are loved by God, and in him we live and move and have our being.

Jackie Harris, Editor

Times to celebrate and rest

Chris Leonard writes:

Happy New Year! Yes, I know it's not the beginning of January, but Jesus would have celebrated New Year in autumn, and in many countries, patterns are set by an academic year starting in September. The good news is that we're looking at God's wise instructions about the patterns and rhythms he designed for us. They include taking time to rest and to celebrate as well as to work, as laid out in Leviticus 23.

Many people struggle with Leviticus, finding it obscure and wondering how all the commands about Jewish sabbaths, animal sacrifices and ancient agricultural festivals are relevant to Christians today. But remember what Jesus said: 'Are you tired? Worn out? Burned out on religion? Come to me. Get away with me and you'll recover your life. I'll show you how to take a real rest. Walk with me and work with me – watch how I do it. Learn the unforced rhythms of grace. I won't lay anything heavy or ill-fitting on you. Keep company with me and you'll learn to live freely and lightly' (Matthew 11:28–30, MSG). Let's keep those 'unforced rhythms of grace' in mind as we read on. The Father's heart was full of grace towards humanity as he gave the instructions recorded in Leviticus, knowing that we need structure for our lives. Remember the sense of lost-ness and chaos during the Covid-19 lockdowns when many of the regular rhythms of life ceased? It's God's grace, his gift as well as his desire, that we take time to celebrate and to rest, as well as to work.

Years ago, I borrowed *The Heavenly Party* (Lion Hudson, 2007), a book by vicar's wife Michele Guinness, who had grown up in a practising Jewish family. Missing the colour and fun, the lively coming together of Jewish family and community for celebration and faith woven right into life, Michele and her husband found ways to incorporate those things into their family and parish year. I recall thinking how much Christians can learn from Jewish festivals and sabbaths, even if Leviticus does make them sound prescriptive, boring and irrelevant. Christians too have been guilty of turning Sundays into boring, legalistic no-fun days – and of failing to understand what God means by rest.

Researching and writing these notes has been thought-provoking and stimulating. I hope you'll find the same as you read and pray through them.

Rhythms and rest

'There are six days when you may work, but the seventh day is a day of sabbath rest, a day of sacred assembly. You are not to do any work; wherever you live, it is a sabbath to the Lord.' (NIV)

Rhythm is built into creation – regular patterns of day and night, seasons of abundance and scarcity, our breaths, heartbeats and natural responses to music's inviting beat. God, who set all these rhythms going and created us in his image, knows why we need rhythms of life, including festivals and anniversaries, work then recreation to replenish.

God's fourth commandment is to work for six days and enjoy holy rest on the seventh (Exodus 20:11). This is because God did the same. After creating everything in six days, God looked at what he'd made and pronounced it complete and 'very good' (Genesis 1:31). The next day he rested, blessing and making everything holy (Genesis 2:2–3).

God's instruction to rest extends beyond one day in seven, though. His command to refrain from working applied to every festival listed in Leviticus 23 – even to those lasting a week! Elsewhere the Bible stipulates three festivals that required all Jewish men to travel to Jerusalem. Jesus went with his whole family – and most of Nazareth. Three days travel each way meant 13 sociable days in all. Taken with weekly sabbaths, that's a lot of annual 'holy days' (a.k.a holidays) with work strictly prohibited. Most of the world would have been toiling every waking hour. God said: 'Rest. Enjoy.'

It all went wrong when religious leaders concocted endless pernickety rules around 'not working'. When human legalism lacked all compassion and understanding, making sabbaths miserable and un-God-like, Jesus objected: 'The sabbath was made for man, not man for the sabbath. So the Son of Man is Lord even of the sabbath' (Mark 2:27–28). God's command to rest never changed! The spirit of it still applies to those of us who are living under the new covenant.

'There remains, then, a sabbath-rest for the people of God; for anyone who enters God's rest also rests from their works, just as God did from his. Let us, therefore, make every effort to enter that rest' (Hebrews 4:9–11).

CHRIS LEONARD

Compassion and remembrance

'Remember that you were slaves in Egypt and that the Lord your God brought you out of there with a mighty hand and an outstretched arm. Therefore the Lord your God has commanded you to observe the sabbath day.' (NIV)

Remembering how God rescued us demands obedience, rest and thankfulness. Deuteronomy's angle on sabbath rest also demands our compassion and justice for those who are still enslaved. So how do we, today, embrace the full richness of God's gift in commanding we take times of rest?

Some Christians advocate the regular setting aside of a few hours – or even a whole day – every week, as God's gift of sabbath rest, joy and replenishment. This intentional use of time to remember God and all he's done saves us from slavery to the cultures that surround us – the driven-ness and greed, the self-obsession, aggressive competition and addictive crutches. Sabbaths free up time to spend with our families, to come together and build community, to enjoy nature and God's world, and to enjoy simply being with him. There's time for creativity, time to sing, party and celebrate; and time to be quiet, to pause and, laying the cares of a normal day aside, to quietly listen to God.

You might like to look up a poem: 'Son-days', by Welsh doctor Henry Vaughan (1621–95). It's available online or you may find it in the library in a book of metaphysical poetry. Like well-cut gemstones, each phrase illuminates different aspects of God's gift of times for sabbath rest. Take time with each phrase and listen to what God has to say to you through them.

Perhaps you could pray for those who find it difficult to plan in times of rest or who are unable to do so. For example, those whose bosses make constant demands on their time, those who work in jobs where they have to be on call, such as farmers and doctors, those who have caring responsibilities for children or other relatives which leaves little time for themselves, and those caught up in the horrors of modern slavery.

Lord, help me find the freedom to set aside time to seek you and all that is of eternal value. Show me how to pray and work with you towards freedom for those trapped in forms of modern slavery. Amen

CHRIS LEONARD

Solemn feasts – trumpets and atonement

'Hold a sacred assembly and deny yourselves, and present a food offering to the Lord. Do not do any work on that day, because it is the Day of Atonement, when atonement is made for you before the Lord your God.' (NIV)

Before the year's final harvest, the Festival of Trumpets is announced by shofars (a 'trumpet' made from a ram's horn). In modern Judaism, ten days of penitence, fasting and prayer then lead up to the holiest day of the year – Yom Kippur, the Day of Atonement, when inadvertent sins are forgiven and the people's relationship with God is restored – hence 'At-One-Ment'. That period sounds remarkably like the Christian Lent, which melds the intentions behind both atonement and that other great Jewish celebration, Passover. Solemnity and celebration can go together, as when Christians celebrate Mass, Holy Communion or Eucharist (which means thanksgiving.)

Both Christians and Jews believe in atonement, with sacrifice at its centre, but they differ too. The book of Hebrews explains: 'Only the high priest entered the inner room, and that only once a year, and never without blood, which he offered for himself and for the sins the people had committed in ignorance' (Hebrews 9:7). Christians believe that as both high priest and sacrificial blood, Jesus atoned for all of our sins, forever.

What do Jews do now about the sacrifices listed in Leviticus? Since the destruction of Jerusalem's temple in AD70, there's no appointed place for them to happen. Apparently, prayer, giving (of money and oneself in good deeds) and study of the Torah substitute for sacrifices given in the temple.

Both Christians and Jews celebrate atonement bringing forgiveness, relief from guilt and even a new start in our relationship with God. When sunset ends on the Jewish Day of Atonement, one single, far-carrying blast of the shofar announces that all is done, for the year that is passed. The festival that follows just five days later is altogether more joyful.

Lord, thank you for solemn celebrations – for Lent and Good Friday, as well as Easter Sunday. We're awed by how you lifted our weight of shame and guilt, sacrificing everything to restore our 'at-one-ment' with you. Amen

CHRIS LEONARD

Autumn – the Festival of Tabernacles

'Live in temporary shelters for seven days… so that your descendants will know that I made the Israelites live in temporary shelters when I brought them out of Egypt. I am the Lord your God.' (NIV)

Five days after the Day of Atonement, the Festival of Tabernacles celebrates autumnal provision: 'After you have gathered the crops of the land, celebrate the festival to the Lord for seven days' (v. 39). Including two sabbaths, this festival lasts for eight multipurpose days – a lengthy holiday resting from work while celebrating 'harvest home' (or 'in-gathering'). The festival commemorates God's miraculous provision of life's essentials – food, drink and shelter – during Israel's 40 years of wilderness wanderings.

Since English October weather is not the best for temporary shelter-dwelling, one year our neighbours' Rabbi asked synagogue members to build improvised frameworks decorated with fresh vegetables in their gardens. They would eat occasional meals in these veggie palaces but sleep in their houses. Our neighbours invited me to join them in the garden where their Rabbi, along with others from their synagogue, had heaped tables with food. Their celebrations were noisy, sociable and very inclusive – of me, a Gentile Christian, and of ten children bouncing on a handy trampoline between their turns at waving the 'Lulav'. It consists of 'branches from luxuriant trees' (v. 40), which represent the fertile land of God's promise. 'Will you wave the Lulav?' the Rabbi asked me. 'Simply turn, praying silently that all to the north, south, east and west have enough to eat next year.' How refreshing! How delightful!

I've enjoyed several Christianised 'Tabernacle services' too. A lovely Roman Catholic priest used to invite all the local churches to a richly creative celebration. Remembering God's provision to Israel – and to us – we danced waving luxuriant branches, dabbled our hands in water basins, ate grapes from baskets handed around by children, listened to Bible stories and sang, praising God, our senses saturated. So colourful, so memorable, so unifying and joyful – I wish more Christians celebrated like that!

Lord, we pray for those without adequate shelter, for the homeless and the refugees. We pray for those with insufficient food, clean water, sanitation, medicine or heating. Lord, have mercy! Amen

CHRIS LEONARD

Solemn repentance to joyous strength

All the people had been weeping as they listened to the words of the law. Nehemiah said, 'Go and enjoy choice food and sweet drinks… Do not grieve, for the joy of the Lord is your strength'… 'Be still, for this is a holy day. Do not grieve.' (NIV)

Because Israel kept breaking their covenant relationship, God exiled them from Jerusalem in order that they might repent. After years in Babylon, another superpower allowed them to return to Jerusalem. Isaiah had prophesied both exile and a joyous, miraculous return; but they found the place in ruins. Vulnerable to attack, they embarked on the hard slog of rebuilding.

But there was more to restore than simply walls, houses and the temple. Until the scriptures or 'law' was read to them, the people had forgotten all about God's wisdom for living and about the national festivals he'd ordained. They repented, weeping, but the Day of Atonement had just passed and now was the time for the Feast of Tabernacles. Their governor, Nehemiah, said, 'This day is holy to the Lord your God. Do not mourn or weep', and the priests also told the people, 'Be still, for this is a holy day. Do not grieve' (vv. 9, 11).

Preparing great banquets and distributing food means hard work – so much for rest and stillness! Yet those days of worshipping God and living in temporary shelters did rest them from all the rebuilding and put their worrying on pause. Their relationship with God restored, they learnt to trust him again and their spirits knew peace.

However, after the festival further repentance was needed. Jerusalem wasn't what it had been. They still had plenty of work to do and much to mourn, but the joy of the Lord remained their strength. Having recognised their own weakness and their dependence on God, they rediscovered trust in his unfailing love and found the space once more to be still and to rejoice.

Lord, when everything around seems dark, difficult, worrying or sad; when guilt overwhelms us and repentance is hard, may we remember to celebrate and worship you so that we can be lifted above ourselves by your joy. Amen
CHRIS LEONARD

Spring – firstfruits and giving

'When you enter the land I am going to give you and you reap its harvest, bring to the priest a sheaf of the first grain you harvest. He is to wave the sheaf before the Lord so it will be accepted on your behalf.' (NIV)

The spring-time Festival of Firstfruits happened after harvesting the winter crop of barley and celebrated the first fruits of the agricultural year. It began the 'counting of the weeks' until the major Festival of Weeks, also known as Pentecost.

The principle of giving first fruits to the Lord applied throughout the year, benefitting priests and Levites who lacked an allocation of land on which to grow their own crops. Numbers 18:12 explains: 'Finest olive oil and all the finest new wine and grain they give to the Lord as the firstfruits of their harvest.' Priests also received 'the first offspring of every womb, both human and animal, that is offered to the Lord … But you must redeem every firstborn son' (Numbers 18:15). Accordingly, after his dedication in the temple, Jesus was 'redeemed' as firstborn son, with the sacrifices prescribed (Luke 2:22–24).

If the ancient Festival of Firstfruits seems comparatively minor, the principle behind it remains vital. God has given us everything, so when his gifts come to fruition, it's only fitting to return the exciting initial results to him, rather than keep them for our own betterment. Giving away our garden's first crop of fruit or vegetables does feel special to me but, even if we haven't grown gifts ourselves, giving them demonstrates an attitude of gratitude and trust over God's generosity towards us.

Here's a thought: 1 Corinthians 15:20 has Christ's resurrection as the first fruits, while James 1:17–18 says: 'Every good and perfect gift is from above… the Father… chose to give us birth through the word of truth, that we might be a kind of firstfruits of all he created.' If we are the first fruits of God's (new) creation, maybe both Jesus and we, in different ways, are living sacrifices and signs of hope?

Lord, everything I have comes from you. Speak to me about my attitude concerning generosity. Help me give more creatively and live more sacrificially. Amen

CHRIS LEONARD

The Festival of Weeks

'Will the Lord be pleased with thousands of rams, with ten thousand rivers of oil?… What does the Lord require of you? To act justly and to love mercy and to walk humbly with your God'. (NIV)

This late spring festival celebrates the final grain harvest of the year, that of wheat, and again involves sacrifices. Its alternative names derive from counting seven weeks (or 50 days) from Firstfruits to Weeks/Pentecost. Instructions to leave crops at the field-edges for the poor to gather show God's concern for social justice, which we see outworked in the book of Ruth.

Unlike Firstfruits, the Festival of Weeks was one of the three great pilgrimage feasts, during which all Jews (men, at least) came together to offer sacrifices in the Jerusalem temple (Exodus 34:23–24). That is why Acts 2:1, 5 says: 'When the day of Pentecost came… there were staying in Jerusalem God-fearing Jews from every nation under heaven.' They all heard Peter's sermon, each, miraculously, in his own language – and the church was born. This coming together would have involved much travel, effort, organisation and expense, especially when you consider that the other two pilgrim festivals, Tabernacles and Passover, each lasted a week – but Pentecost only 24 hours.

Aromas from cooking bread, beef, lamb and even goat must have pleased the priests and delighted the people, especially after all that travelling. I think God would have enjoyed the people coming all that way to worship and thank him. He would have enjoyed the cohesion and bonding cemented through these great gatherings as his people shared communal meals and fellowship in their camps around Jerusalem. Their leaving gleanings for the poor would have pleased him too. But Micah shows how religion and even sacrifices can become perverted, producing a foul stench rather than a pleasing aroma.

Lord, I'm reminded of 1 Corinthians 13:3 (ESV): 'If I give away all I have, and if I deliver up my body to be burned, but have not love, I gain nothing.' Help me know – and do – what pleases you. Amen

CHRIS LEONARD

The Festival of Passover

'Obey these instructions as a lasting ordinance for you and your descendants... When your children ask you, "What does this ceremony mean to you?" then tell them, "It is the Passover sacrifice to the Lord, who passed over the houses of the Israelites... when he struck down the Egyptians."' (NIV)

The great pilgrim festival of Passover lasts seven days in spring, with First-fruits on its second day. It celebrates God rescuing Israel from slavery and foreshadows Jesus, who enjoyed the Seder (or Passover) meal with close friends before his crucifixion. Christians re-enact Jesus' last meal, using bread and wine to reflect upon and remember his death as Passover's sacrificial lamb. Jews re-enact the slaughter of lambs whose blood, daubed on their doorways, warned God's avenging angel to spare their firstborn. They then had to leave in such haste that bread had no time to rise, hence the alternative name: Feast of Unleavened Bread (bread made without yeast).

One year, the churches in my village organised a Seder (Passover) meal together on Maundy Thursday. We too ate Matzos (unleavened bread) and bitter herbs (to represent slavery's misery); we drank the different cups, each with their special prayer – everything so symbolic! Though we celebrated together, Jews eat Seder meals in individual households of extended families with several generations present. Small children are encouraged throughout to ask the meaning of everything eaten, drunk, said and done. God's involvement in their collective history becomes a very present and memorable part of their young lives.

Christians also remember and celebrate what Jesus has done, rescuing us from slavery to sin and making us his family, his people. We too use things we can touch, taste and smell in our sacrament of Eucharist, but do we make God's love tangible to children? Most exclude them from our celebration meal. Maybe we can't give them bread and wine, but in what other ways could we draw them into our collective experience of the reality of God at our festivals – without involving chocolate eggs or endless presents?

Lord, there's so much we can learn from Jewish celebrations. Inspire us and show us how to enliven our own celebrations with the vibrant, unmissable sounds, tastes and colours of heaven. Amen

CHRIS LEONARD

Jesus on celebration and rest

'Bring the fattened calf and kill it. Let's have a feast and celebrate. For this my son was dead and is alive again; he was lost and is found.' So they began to celebrate. (NIV)

I've been to some great parties and some dreadful ones. The latter seemed to be more about taking than giving, about showing off or drinking too much, about satisfying lust instead of nurturing friendships. The younger son in Jesus' story experienced both kinds, while his brother couldn't bring himself to celebrate at all. Rediscovering something precious, the woman and farmer in Jesus' other two parables in our reading celebrated exuberantly.

Jesus told these three stories in response to the religious leaders' mutterings about his welcoming sinners and eating with them. He certainly celebrated, providing an abundance of superb wine for a wedding (John 2:1–10). He also taught about God's generosity when he told a story about a man who arranged a lavish feast. When those on his guest-list had something better to do, he invited needy strangers instead (Luke 14:15–24). I wonder who will be at his stupendous party at the climax of the Bible's great saga of salvation? Revelation 19:9 says of it: 'Blessed are those who are invited to the wedding supper of the Lamb!'

To bring about any celebration takes time and effort, it costs and, depending on age and energy levels, we tire. Even Jesus had to get away sometimes from constant demands on his wisdom, healing or rescue. He made time to be alone, to be replenished and to communicate with his Father. He read the scriptures, attended synagogue, relaxed with friends, walked and observed nature.

So, when are we to rest, work or celebrate? Luke 10:38–42 might help. When Jesus and friends needed food, someone had to prepare it. Martha obliged. Perhaps she could have worried less and made things simpler, but in fact Jesus called her out for finding fault with her sister Mary for not helping. Suppose God tells me to work and my 'sister' to rest – how do I react?

Jesus, if I'm a driven person, seldom truly resting or celebrating, help me to follow your example. May we all find your celebration joy as our strength, rest and replenishment – our springboards to worship and to serve you. Amen
CHRIS LEONARD

Women at work in the Bible

Tanya Marlow writes:

When someone asks us, 'What do you do?', we so often answer with our job title: 'I'm a receptionist.' That alone shows how much of our identity we associate with our work. I've wrestled with this issue over the decades as I've dealt with Myalgic Encephalomyelitis, a chronic illness meaning I have very little energy. Most of my day is spent lying in bed and maybe watching some TV. I also write Christian books and deliver lectures and conference talks online, so this gives me part of an identity: I'm a writer, a lecturer and a speaker. When we look at the Bible, however, there's no such obsession with what type of job we do. What is the Bible concerned with, then?

To discover the answer to that question, we're going to consider women at work in the Bible. Here are three things to observe in the next two weeks.

1. The women's work is incredibly varied. Contrary to our perceptions of ancient women staying at home and cooking, most women in the Bible had careers. In the studies that follow, we see a wide variety of roles: political leaders, carers, models, artists, farmers. People like Sarai and Abigail were wealthy, worked alongside their husbands and were senior managers. We also see unemployed and exploited women, as there are today. For each study, even if you are not working in that particular field, you can pray for others in that situation.

2. Work is broader than what we're paid to do. Nowadays, we define work too narrowly as employment. The Bible has a wider perspective. Cooking at home is a type of work; looking after children is work; giving to charity is work. It all matters, so bear this in mind for application, especially if you're unemployed, retired or at home with children.

3. We're not what we do: we're how we do it. This is the biggest lesson. The Bible is less interested in our activity than the type of person we are while we're doing it. What you'll discover is that these biblical women faced the same challenges of justice, sexism, morality and frustration at work as we do. These challenges and ethical dilemmas revealed and formed their character. These women offer practical wisdom for us today, and I'm excited to share that with you.

'What's my calling?' (Eve)

God blessed them, and God said to them, 'Be fruitful and multiply, and fill the earth and subdue it; and have dominion over the fish of the sea and over the birds of the air and over every living thing that moves upon the earth.' (NRSV)

In my 20s, I agonised over my calling. I didn't just want a job but something with meaning and purpose. Drawn to theology and Christian ministry, I eventually had a perfect lecturing job, training those who felt called to ministry. I had found my vocation.

However, ten years later, I got ill and became housebound. I couldn't work at all. My ideas of calling were obliterated. I realised that much of what I thought calling was – enjoying a job that fitted my skills and passion – was a luxury few have. Most people, certainly on a global scale, don't find their calling within their jobs, which are often menial or mediocre. Their calling is necessarily broader: how they live their lives and relate to others.

Whenever we're wondering about our Calling-with-a-capital-C or lamenting the lack of a satisfying job, it can help to remind ourselves that calling is far broader than paid employment. Loving God and others, caring for those on low incomes, welcoming refugees – God calls all of us to this and more, and it's exciting and important work.

According to our passage today, ecology is also at the heart of our calling. Genesis 1 tells us that women and men are equal partners in caring for the world (vv. 26–27). The first commands were to look after the creatures of the earth and ensure the next generation of humanity (v. 28). Resources were distributed fairly among earth's inhabitants – humans got the fruit and animals got the green plants (vv. 29–30). Environmental concerns aren't an optional extra in God's economy but central to our responsibility as humans and Christians.

Today, whatever your job, consider that first calling, to look after the world, its animals and the next generation of humans. How are you fulfilling that calling?

Lord, help us to do small things that produce big change. Where possible, enable us to share resources fairly, campaign for better ecology and animal welfare, nurture young people and leave the world a better place. Amen

TANYA MARLOW

'My work is hard' (Eve)

'Cursed is the ground because of you; in toil you shall eat of it all the days of your life; thorns and thistles it shall bring forth for you; and you shall eat the plants of the field.' (NRSV)

For a while, we lived in a house with an apple tree in the garden. The fruit came faithfully each year. However, one year it yielded no fruit at all. It was baffling, and I was sad to lose our apple crumble supply that year. Then, I read in the paper that it wasn't just us: farmers up and down the country had lost their entire crop and there was a nationwide shortage of apples. As I thought about my one apple tree, I considered the powerlessness and fear the farmers must have felt. All their hard work resulted in nothing.

Today's passage reveals the consequences of humanity's sin against God. Genesis 2:15, where the humans are instructed to 'till' and 'keep' the trees, shows us that even in the idyllic garden of Eden, work is still present. Crucially, work is enjoyable. After the fall, the tilling becomes toil. Note that although there are consequences for the humans, only the serpent (v. 14) and the ground (v. 17) are specifically cursed. Humans would have to eat field plants, like the animals. Even today, we must work hard in order to eat. If you have a physical element to your job, or are dependent on weather and crops, you will particularly identify with the sweat (v. 19) and utter frustration of it all.

To everyone who works to the point of exhaustion, especially physically, this is a reminder that God never wanted the experience of work to be that way. If work feels hard and miserable when we feel we're supposed to enjoy a job, it's because it really is hard, and we were designed for better work. It's not about pretending it's good. Rather, we give the frustration to our compassionate God, asking daily for his comfort, strength and presence as we persevere.

If your work is hard: *Jesus, you once slept on a storm-wracked boat because of exhaustion. Minister to me and strengthen my weary body and soul.* If you benefit from others' labour: *May my purchases promote justice in the world.*

TANYA MARLOW

'Younger people are taking our jobs' (Sarai)

But Abram said to Sarai, 'Your slave-girl is in your power; do to her as you please.' Then Sarai dealt harshly with her, and she ran away from her. (NRSV)

At first glance, Abram's coercive sex with a slave to force her to be a surrogate doesn't seem to connect with our theme of work. Primarily, this is about the horrors of slavery, which still continue to this day, so I must emphasise that the main application of this passage is fighting against today's slave trade. However, there are principles in the passage that can be loosely mapped on to the world of work. Sarai, the rich owner, is in charge of Hagar. Fearing she couldn't fulfil her role as child bearer, she outsources it to the younger generation for free labour. When Hagar is successful, Sarai despises and abuses her, while Abram gives his tacit permission. It is a horrific story, and God condemns their impatience and abuse.

Though we're not directly involved in slavery, we can still be tempted to mistreat employees or resent the next generation. It's a familiar pattern made popular by films like *The Devil Wears Prada* and Sandra Bullock's *The Proposal*: the boss feels threatened by the assistant and abuses them.

It raises challenging questions: you may love the person you're mentoring while you're mentoring them, but how do you feel when their success surpasses yours? Is there an employee who just really annoys you, and you know in your heart you don't treat them as fairly as the other employees? Even if you don't work, have you ever felt less significant or less valued, either because you're too old or too young? Do you resent another generation for their advantages?

When Sarai lost her trust in God's goodness towards her, she left her path and abused others. Today, I examine my heart for jealousy and ask God to reassure me of my own path to follow. I invite you to do similarly.

Father, we come to you with our hurts, resentments and fears about our career and future. Where we have uncertainty, show us your trustworthiness. Where we are jealous, fill us with your reassurance. Guide us, we pray. Amen
TANYA MARLOW

'My boss hates me' (Hagar)

And God heard the voice of the boy, and the angel of God called to Hagar from heaven, and said to her, 'What troubles you, Hagar? Do not be afraid; for God has heard the voice of the boy where he is.' (NRSV)

My friend trained for several years to be a medic in a prestigious hospital. It had long been her dream, and the work itself was extremely fulfilling. However, the work environment became increasingly toxic. Her boss demanded more hours for the same pay and created a culture where efficiency and profit were valued over patient safety. Internally, she was conflicted – wanting to both please her boss and care for her patients. Eventually, it started affecting her physical and mental health, and with great sadness she resigned.

Hagar knows all about working in a toxic environment. Her first reaction is to leave, but when she's in the wilderness God tells her to return and submit to Sarai (16:9–10). After enduring for several years, she's eventually kicked out because of Sarai's jealousy and meets God in the wilderness again. This time Hagar stays away.

Why did God initially tell Hagar to return to an abusive situation? There is a clue given in Abram's ages in the two passages (16:16, 21:5). When Hagar initially ran away, she was pregnant. Out in the desert, she and Ishmael, alone, would likely have died. By the time she leaves for good, Ishmael is 14, which is technically an adult in that culture. He was now safe, and God blessed Ishmael and his descendants (21:20–21). There was a time for Hagar to stay and a time to go, and God orchestrated both.

Generally, if someone is in an abusive situation, I would advise them to leave. But in situations where it's not so clear cut, we need God's wisdom in the timing of when to stay or go. Either way, Hagar's story teaches us that God cares deeply about our work environments and wants us to flourish and thrive.

(Pray this for yourself or a friend.) *Faithful God, it's so hard to know why our situations are so hard. Give us either the strength to stay, or the courage and opportunity to leave. Show us the path, O Lord. Amen*

TANYA MARLOW

'My boss wants me to do something immoral' (Shiphrah and Puah)

But the midwives feared God; they did not do as the king of Egypt commanded them, but they let the boys live. (NRSV)

Imprisoned in the Auschwitz concentration camp, a Christian midwife was tasked with delivering babies – then immediately drowning them. Her life was at risk if she refused. However, she stood up to the infamous Nazi doctor, Josef Mengele, and refused. Somehow, she was spared. She delivered around 3,000 babies. Historian Tim Dowley tells her story in his recent book, *Defying the Holocaust* (SPCK, 2020).

Her experience was eerily similar to a predicament faced by midwives three millennia ago. In a country run by a racist tyrant who did not tolerate defiance, Shiphrah and Puah disobeyed their boss' orders.

In the text, we see how much God valued the courage of these women. They are specially named in the annals of history (v. 15), God treated them well (v. 20) and gave them families of their own (v. 21), implying they were previously either single or infertile. In their defiance, they were also shrewd, and protected themselves as best possible through their humorous excuse for why the Hebrew babies were still alive. Their lie was the far lesser of two evils.

The story shows us two women at work who refused to do something deeply immoral, risking their livelihood and safety in the process, because they feared God more than humans. In our daily work, we also face ethical choices. Sometimes it means advocating for policy change. Lizzie, a friend of mine who is a midwife today, is educating midwives about perineal trauma to change future birthing practice. Another friend at a bank refused to market expensive products to customers who would go into debt. It might mean speaking up for a colleague. We are to be righteous and shrewd. Though it's costly and lonely to do things differently, God sees your sacrifice, and your actions could potentially change the course of history.

Lord, it's so easy to justify immoral actions when everyone else is doing it and our career is on the line if we don't follow suit. Give courage today to anyone who needs to stand up to their boss for the sake of justice. Amen

TANYA MARLOW

'My creative work feels unimportant' (Miriam)

Then the prophet Miriam, Aaron's sister, took a tambourine in her hand; and all the women went out after her with tambourines and with dancing. And Miriam sang to them: 'Sing to the Lord, for he has triumphed gloriously; horse and rider he has thrown into the sea.' (NRSV)

In our society, creative workers are usually respected, but underpaid. Most creative people can't make a living from their art and must squeeze it in among their other roles. I have a friend who makes money from being a delivery driver, but that's not what his identity or calling is: he is an artist. It's easy to feel that if there is no money to be made, then there is no point in doing the work. Moses and Miriam show us otherwise.

The Israelites had survived years of slavery, then ten plagues and Pharaoh's worsening cruelty. Finally, they had been set free. As Moses led them out via a supernatural path through the Red Sea, they felt victorious. Then they looked behind in horror: the Egyptian army was coming. They would all be slaughtered. Today we read two songs about the miraculous moment God saved the Israelites from certain death. The refrain in both is, 'Horse and rider he has thrown into the sea.' It's God's power that's emphasised. God was their warrior. The glory goes to God.

Despite the urgency of their situation, the Israelites paused to replay the story and celebrate. When momentous things happen to us, we need times of lament or celebration – and we need artists to lead us. Wonderfully, Miriam didn't let Moses' song stop her from adding her own song, and she led a community in percussion and dance. The world needs our unique voices. If you are feeling discouraged by your creative work, remember that Moses and Miriam's songs and stories were sung for hundreds of years afterwards (Psalm 77, 78, 114, Isaiah 43:16–17, 51). God used them to teach future generations about God's goodness. Keep singing your songs.

Lord, thank you for the storytellers, artists, performers, musicians, designers and other creative people. Sustain them. May we hear their prophecy and make time to celebrate God's power in our lives. Amen

TANYA MARLOW

'When do I speak up about discrimination in the workplace?' (Miriam)

While they were at Hazeroth, Miriam and Aaron spoke against Moses because of the Cushite woman whom he had married (for he had indeed married a Cushite woman). (NRSV)

I recently read Austin Channing Brown's bestseller, *I'm Still Here: Black dignity in a world made for whiteness* (Virago Press, 2020). Austin's parents gave her a white man's name because they knew in a racist and sexist world that would give her the best chance of getting a job interview. Though most workplaces may not be known for overt racism, committing microaggressions of racism can still be a destructive reality.

Austin's typical workday included colleagues getting her confused with the other black employees and questioning both her manner and quality of work. Living in a world that discriminates against you takes its toll. Though Austin is American, British black Christian writers Ben Lindsay, Chine McDonald and Azariah France-Williams confirm the situation is as bad here.

Though she started off well as a prophet, Miriam committed the sin of racism: she spoke against Moses for marrying a black woman. Descending from Noah's son Ham, the Cushites, south of Egypt, were known for their dark black skin. In Exodus 2, Moses married Zipporah who was a Midianite (around Saudi Arabia). This Cushite wife is likely Moses' second wife, perhaps following Zipporah's death. The Israelites were not universally forbidden to marry foreigners, only specific nations with detestable practices (Deuteronomy 7:1–6; Ezra 9:1). Including other peoples into the community of Israelites was always part of God's plan (for example, Exodus 12:37–38).

Miriam temporarily receives a disfiguring skin disease as God is so angry; it's a glimpse into being shunned for one's appearance. Racism, sexism, homophobia and ableism still exist in the workplace, and they offend God. Though it takes courage to rock the boat, we should be the first to speak up.

Lord, please awaken me to the sins of prejudice in my own heart and give me courage to protest when I see other people's subtle bigotry. For those being discriminated against: *Lord, direct my holy anger in righteous ways. Amen*

TANYA MARLOW

'Why don't I get paid what I'm worth?' (Daughters of Zelophehad)

And the Lord spoke to Moses, saying: 'The daughters of Zelophehad are right in what they are saying; you shall indeed let them possess an inheritance among their father's brothers and pass the inheritance of their father on to them.' (NRSV)

Venus Williams made history by playing outstanding tennis. However, she also made history by asking for a pay rise. Continuing Billie Jean King's campaign for equal pay in the tennis grand slams, the turning point came when Venus wrote an opinion piece for *The Times* in 2006. Under pressure, both Wimbledon and the French Open announced that the following year, the pay would be equal for male and female competitors.

Here in Numbers, five women went boldly to Moses to request equal pay. Women weren't allowed an inheritance, but this would have left them in penury and ended their father's line. Rather than decide himself, Moses took it to the Lord in prayer, as we should do for such decisions. God's answer was clear. Not only would these women receive their inheritance (v. 7), but their actions would create a principle for all (vv. 8–10) and would be a lasting ordinance (v. 11). Mahlah, Noah, Hoglah, Milcah and Tirzah asked to be seen as equals and, in so doing, they changed history.

Today, there is still a gender pay gap – the Office for National Statistics states that in 2021 the median pay was 15% less for women than for men. Though it might seem selfish or un-Christian to ask for better pay or conditions, we see that through asking for themselves, the five daughters secured justice for women for generations afterwards. For those who don't get paid for their work, it might be about appealing unfair benefit decisions, or simply requesting full respect from family and friends for your role in life. God loves justice for women. As you think of your own situation, consider too the wider world, where women often labour in inhumane conditions.

Pray about whether you need to ask for better pay or conditions, or treat your employees better. Explore organisations such as the Clean Clothes Campaign and the Fair Wear Foundation for better conditions for garment workers.

TANYA MARLOW

'How do I lead well in a man's world?' (Deborah)

At that time Deborah, a prophetess, wife of Lappidoth, was judging Israel. She used to sit under the palm of Deborah between Ramah and Bethel in the hill country of Ephraim; and the Israelites came up to her for judgement. (NRSV)

At the time of the Judges, much like our world today, society was immoral, and God's people had grown complacent. The pattern throughout Judges was that God alerted the Israelites to their sin through foreign attack; the Israelites begged God for help; then God raised a military 'deliverer' for them who conquered the enemy army. Following their battle, the winning warrior would rule, or 'judge', over Israel, until they died. The leaders were morally flawed: Gideon was reluctant to trust God, Abimelech killed his 70 brothers and Samson's vanity led to his downfall.

This is why Deborah shines as distinctive in this environment. The only female judge, she isn't a 'deliverer': she rules over Israel before any major battle. She's primarily a prophet, so she doesn't need to prove anything by force. She merely listens to the Lord and passes on his messages and judgements. No riches for her; she sits under a tree.

When the battle finally comes, she delegates, according to God's instruction. Rather than leading an army herself, she summons Barak to answer God's call to rescue them. He hesitates and begs for her presence. This should not be viewed too harshly, because asking a prophet to accompany you is asking for God's presence. Seeing his motive for self-aggrandisement, however, she emphasises that this is about salvation for Israel, not personal accomplishment. She is Israel's judge, not him. A random woman, Jael, betraying her husband, kills the oppressor; Barak defeats the army; Deborah leads and prophesies. Ultimately, God gets the glory.

Deborah shows a better way of leading to all. She listens to God, follows her own path, isn't seeking power and is unafraid to delegate to others. Let us lead as Deborah did and ask God to produce leaders like her.

Ask yourself: how am I like Deborah, secure in God's calling? Or like Barak, hungry for glory? Pray for our leaders, both state and church. May God crush the Siseras, humble the Baraks and anoint the Deborahs.

TANYA MARLOW

'What if I can't earn money?' (Naomi)

She said to them, 'Call me no longer Naomi, call me Mara, for the Almighty has dealt bitterly with me. I went away full, but the Lord has brought me back empty; why call me Naomi…?' (NRSV)

I have a friend who lives alone. She's unable to work because of chronic illness, and the meagre amount she gets from benefits leaves her very vulnerable. Keeping warm is a challenge in winter. She can't cook for herself, so she buys ready meals. For her, a treat is one fresh apple per week.

Naomi was in a similar position after the death of her husband and two sons. Left penniless and unable to work, she begged her former friends to change her name from 'pleasant' to 'bitter' (1:20–21). However, she was not entirely empty: she had Ruth, her Moabite daughter-in-law. There were no overt miracles here – instead, God provided for Naomi through Ruth's hard physical labour in a menial job (2:7) and a rich patron who artificially bumped up Ruth's wages (2:14–16). Without this combination, particularly Boaz's role, Naomi may just have been another statistic of older people who died from poverty. Instead, God gave her people who would look after her, even into her old age.

We have plenty of Naomis in society today. You may be one. Being unemployed is hard enough: it's lonely and we are built for activity. Unemployment with poverty is even harder: life becomes very precarious. It is all too inevitable for despair, depression and even bitterness to set in. The challenge for us, as for Naomi, is to spot God's hand at work in our lives, looking out for God's blessing. Naomi rose to that challenge, recognising that Boaz's generosity was also God's kindness to her, and she prayed for Boaz to be blessed (2:20). If you're a Naomi, know that God loves you and is your provider. And the challenge for Ruth and Boaz was to be the answer to Naomi's prayer for provision. So too for us today.

For Naomis: *God, my provider and loving parent, bless me with your kindness. Take away my bitterness and despair. Look after me and restore me. Amen*
For everyone else: *Jesus, may we give generously so others can survive. Amen*

TANYA MARLOW

'I'm always having to cover for other people's messes' (Abigail)

David said to Abigail, 'Blessed be the Lord, the God of Israel, who sent you to meet me today! Blessed be your good sense.' (NRSV)

It was not Abigail's job to be the peacekeeper; it was her husband's. The extremely rich Nabal should have shown gratitude for David's protection of his employees, but he refused. In a culture of honour and shame, this was a deep insult. David decided to get violent revenge on Nabal and all his workers. Abigail's role in all this was simply to be subservient and loyal to her husband, even though he was aptly named as 'Fool'. She may well have been spared and her good-for-nothing husband would have died.

Abigail was not so much protecting herself, or even her husband, through her efficiently prepared feast for 400; she was protecting David. In her speech, she took the blame upon herself, which is a sign of true leadership, and appealed to David's integrity in his own leadership. In the chapters either side of this one, David honourably spares Saul's life rather than seize the throne by force. If David had killed Nabal for his insult, he would be ruining his future rule with 'bloodguilt'. Abigail alone saw this. David was right to bless her good sense, which came in the nick of time. Though she was shrewd, Abigail should also be recognised as devout, even prophetic: she was protecting the future well-being of the whole nation. And God, the just, punished Nabal on David's behalf.

So many times, in work and other areas of life, we're faced with clearing up other people's mess when it's not our job. It's not always right to let lazy people off the hook, but where a job needs to be done for the sake of the work itself or the welfare of others, we must grit our teeth, pray to the Lord, who sees things done in secret, and serve God through it.

Are you always cleaning up other people's messes? Talk to God about it; work through the resentment and frustration; discern the best way forward. (Consider too, whether other people clean up your messes!)

TANYA MARLOW

'Why can't my faith and work be separate?' (Esther)

'Do not think that in the king's palace you will escape any more than all the other Jews. For if you keep silent at such a time as this, relief and deliverance will rise for the Jews from another quarter, but you and your father's family will perish.' (NRSV)

In the truncated versions of John Newton's life, he is known as the hymn writer of 'Amazing Grace' and an outspoken abolitionist. The real story is messier. When Newton became a Christian, he was a people-trafficker. Even when he left a few years later to become ordained, he still invested in the industry. It took him more than 30 years of wrestling with his conscience before he finally spoke out against slavery, deeply ashamed of his part in it.

When Esther initially hears the news about the king's edict to kill the Jews, she's similarly not immediately heroic. Feeling powerless to change anything, she looks to protect herself. The bad things will happen to other people, not her, she reasons (v. 13). While Mordecai is in sackcloth, she gives him new clothes, either to provide for him or (more likely) silence his protest (v. 4). Mordecai is her conscience: she has more positional power than she realises. She must use it to speak up for others, even if it endangers her life (v. 16). Eventually, she agrees.

Both Newton and Esther warn us of the danger of separating our faith from our work life. It's true that, most of the time, when we are working, we're called to focus on that. But there will be times when God puts us in a place 'for such a time as this' and our voice is needed to protect others. If we're not in the workplace, maybe it's about who we speak up for or stay silent about in conversation. I take great comfort in the fact that these two heroes of the faith failed at first. It means it's never too late to do the right thing. Perhaps even today, the Holy Spirit is prompting you about a split in your conscience; take time to listen.

Spend time today thinking through all your work or the various communities you're involved in. Imagine Jesus sitting on the chair next – are there any splits in your conscience with any of those activities and communities?

TANYA MARLOW

'My work never stops' (Martha)

But the Lord answered her, 'Martha, Martha, you are worried and distracted by many things; there is need of only one thing.' (NRSV)

In 2017, a French artist known simply as Emma produced an online comic strip that went viral. It was titled, 'You should've asked', and showed a stereotypical scene where a dad was relaxing with guests for a dinner party while the mum simultaneously juggled feeding the kids and cooking a fancy meal. When the pot boiled over, the dad protested at the mum's frustration: 'If you needed help, you should've asked!'

The mum is expected not only to do most of the tasks but also to be the project manager in remembering what needs to be done, deciding on an action, then planning and delegating the tasks. This extra, unseen work is known as the 'mental load'. Keeping the peace at home is called 'emotional labour'. It's draining and, in a heterosexual marriage, it most often falls to the woman, no matter what her employment status is. Additionally, if you're the only adult in your household, absolutely everything falls on you.

The situation with Martha and Mary could have been made into a similarly popular comic strip. Martha carries the mental load and does all the tasks while Mary abandons her. In a hospitality culture, Mary's response is rude. However, Jesus shocks Martha – and us – by saying that however important these things are, they don't compare to simply being with Jesus.

Jesus' words to Martha are not so much a rebuke as an invitation. When we are in despair, exhausted and frustrated because there's always more to do and it's always us who does it, that is the point to stop, rest and simply be. It's counterintuitive, but being with Jesus brings the refreshment and clarity of thought we need. We can then either carry on or think more creatively about how to divide the mental load and chores in our household.

Lord Jesus, I come to you today with my lists and tasks and feelings of being overwhelmed. May I enjoy your presence today and not rush from it. Please restore me. Amen

TANYA MARLOW

'Does anyone notice my caring work?' (Dorcas)

Now in Joppa there was a disciple whose name was Tabitha, which in Greek is Dorcas. She was devoted to good works and acts of charity. (NRSV)

When we were first dating, my husband Jon gave me relaxing shoulder massages and kissed me on the cheek. When we were married, we joked and laughed as he carried me over the threshold. It was all so romantic. Twenty years on, I yell at Jon in desperation, and he massages my knotted shoulders until my pain gives way to tears of relief and gratitude. He still carries me up flights of stairs, but out of necessity, because I can't climb them. We haven't stopped laughing and joking, though our sense of humour may now be a little darker. Those same actions have different connotations now that I am housebound, but they are no less romantic.

Like Jon, Dorcas was a carer. The phrase translated 'acts of charity' is literally 'works of mercy'. In the gospel of Luke, written by the same person who wrote Acts, the word 'mercy' is always associated with alleviating suffering. Dorcas' ministry of clothing widows and other actions was relieving others' suffering and showing mercy. Whether you are paid to be a carer for a stranger, nurture young children, look after older relatives, help neurodiverse people navigate a neurotypical world or support friends battling ongoing physical or mental illness, it is precious work and echoes Christ's ministry.

Caring work is often unpaid, unseen and unappreciated. Sometimes the people we care for can't show gratitude for what we're doing and are trapped in their own world of struggle, which can be agonising for onlookers. But God sees. Dorcas' work was so valuable that she was resurrected in order to continue it. As a recipient of care, I can say that each time you help someone without indicating resentment, you make that suffering person feel more fully human and loved. May God give you strength to continue it.

Lord, give me a picture of your mercy to me, relieving my suffering, as I help to ease the difficulties of others. Give me grace and gentleness as I do this vital work and sustain me by your Spirit. Amen

TANYA MARLOW

Giants in our lives

Michele D. Morrison writes:

When Covid-19 lockdown rules drove our weekly worship services on to Zoom, our congregation became well-acquainted with Lucy Grimble's song, 'Goliath'. In it, she sings about only needing a small seed of faith. That seed of faith, like the pebbles in David's pouch, is enough to slay the giants which stalk us all.

Not all seeds germinate in the same way. I soak dried peas overnight before planting, but when I plant pumpkin seeds, I put them on edge and cover them with cling film to facilitate sprouting. Some seeds can simply be scattered and still germinate. How do we treat the seed of faith? It's a good idea to soak it in scripture, marinate it in contemplation and cover it in the Spirit.

Jesus taught that faith the size of a mustard seed is enough. You don't need a big faith to slay the giants in your life. You just need a living faith.

When David faced Goliath, he recognised that 'the battle is the Lord's' (1 Samuel 17:47, NIV). David knew and trusted in God's power, in his faithfulness and in his dependability. Over this next fortnight, we will be looking at the tactics David used to defeat Goliath. We'll start by reminding ourselves who God is and how we are told to put on the armour of God and be prepared to fight. Then we will look at several different giants who stalk and harass many of us at one time or another.

At the end of each day's study, there is a verse from scripture which can be spoken out and declared as truth when the pressure is on. Paul wrote to the Ephesians about spiritual warfare and identified the sword of the Spirit as the word of God, the two-edged sword which has power. Speaking God's word out loud is powerful and effective.

David came up against many giants after Goliath, giants like anxiety and fear, depression and guilt, which still confront us today. The Psalms record many battles David took to the Lord and entrusted to him. David knew his Lord, and by faith he slayed his giants. May we all do the same.

The battle belongs to the Lord

'All those gathered here will know that it is not by sword or spear that the Lord saves; for the battle is the Lord's, and he will give all of you into our hands.' (NIV)

Let's unpack this familiar story. David's dad asks him to take some bread and cheese out to his brothers and report back on how the battle is going. As David arrives, he hears the taunts of Goliath. He starts asking questions. His brother Eliab belittles him, but David asserts himself. Saul expresses doubt that David can make a difference, but David defends his credentials and walks out to meet Goliath.

The battle begins before David picks his stone and the victory is his as he voices his trust in the name of God. His faith activates change in the dynamics of the unseen supernatural struggle. The stone hits the sweet spot with deadly precision and Goliath crashes down.

The apostle Paul displays a similar faith and audacity. He declares his total trust in the power of the cross of Christ, first to church leaders in Jerusalem (Acts 9:26–28), then to the Sanhedrin (Acts 23:1–11) and finally he takes on the towering giant of Rome (Acts 28:17–31). He trusts God, and through Paul, faith in Jesus Christ spreads throughout the empire.

Key things to note as we face our own giants:

- Remember whose you are, and who he is. He is the living God, eager for our faltering faith to engage with his prevailing power to defeat the enemy. He is for us, not against us.
- Don't be intimidated by anyone: family, friend or authority. Don't lose heart. It can undermine both our attitude and the outcome. The church is at its best when we encourage and are encouraged by each other.
- Dismiss doubts by actively remembering God's past victories. 'The Lord who rescued me… will rescue me' (v. 37).
- Be prepared: wear the armour of God – the belt of truth, the breastplate of righteousness, shoes of the gospel of peace and the helmet of salvation. Wield the shield of faith and the sword of the Spirit. Be brave.

'The Lord is my light and my salvation – whom shall I fear?' (Psalm 27:1). Lord God, may I be encouraged today to arm myself and run on to the battlefield knowing you run with me. Amen

MICHELE D. MORRISON

Remember, remember!

'The Lord who rescued me from the paw of the lion and the paw of the bear will rescue me from the hand of this Philistine.' (NIV)

In more than 40 years as a Christian, I have seen God answer many prayers for healing. A person who attempted suicide, over whom the doctors declared, 'It's too late; the die is cast', awoke, completely healed. An ovarian cyst which the doctor said 'can't go away without surgery' went away. These were dramatic answers to prayer, and yet my inclination when faced with a serious health concern is often to forget these victories and remember instead the back operation which resulted in pain and a limp or my sister, who succumbed to breast cancer despite prayers and fasting.

Rehearse your blessings. Take time every day to remember God's answers and feed those memories so that their stature eclipses the detritus of disappointments. Whatever memory aids are useful to you – journals, digital bullet-points, Post-it notes on the fridge – use them. What you remember about God's activity in your life is lethal ammunition against a sneering giant.

It is profoundly ungrateful and disrespectful to forget what the Lord has done for us. Moreover, it is disempowering. It's as we remember what the Lord has done for us previously that worship bubbles up and transforms the situation, building faith like a siege ramp against any giant. Our vantage point changes as we worship God and realise the battle is his.

Which giant is stalking you today: addiction, anxiety, anger, despair, low self-esteem, unforgiveness? Is temptation whispering in your ear or cynicism shouting from the rooftops?

David heard Goliath. Listen for and identify the giants in your valleys, so you can target them from the mountaintop of worship. We can defeat them with the high praises of God in our mouths. We can rout them with scripture, the sword of the Spirit, declared aloud with conviction. God has given us armour appropriate for our strength and situation. Prayerfully put it on. Be prepared.

'Finally, be strong in the Lord and in his mighty power' (Ephesians 6:10). 'We live by faith, not by sight' (2 Corinthians 5:7). Focus on Jesus, who never leaves nor forsakes you.

MICHELE D. MORRISON

The giant of fear

We look away from the natural realm and we focus our attention and expectation on to Jesus who birthed faith within us and who leads us forward into faith's perfection. (TPT)

Glen Scrivener wrote: 'Fear is when we're overwhelmed by life. Faith is when we're overwhelmed by God... by his word, by his promise' (*Reading Between the Lines*, 10 Publishing, 2018). What or who we choose to focus on will determine our success in fighting our fears, but we have to keep vigilant.

Jane was walking home after visiting her friend, Ruth. Absent-mindedly, she chose to take a short cut and, as she stepped down a slight incline, she slipped on the mud and broke her ankle badly in two places. At a time when she needed to be active as she prepared to move house, she was laid up with plaster and pins and crutches.

We can't afford absentmindedness with giants on the loose. Focusing on whatever causes you to fear is like leaving a dripping tap at the top of a dirt hill: it creates a lethal slope down which you can slide, incapacitating your faith in Jesus.

We need to ensure that we focus our attention on Jesus (v. 2) because it is by faith in him that we can defeat the fears (giants) in our lives. God told Abram he would protect him, and Abram believed him. Do you? 'Abram believed the Lord, and the Lord counted him as righteous because of his faith' (Genesis 15:6, NLT). Faith in Jesus clothes us in his righteousness and we are safe in God for eternity. There is nothing to fear.

As bombs rained down on their community, Ukrainians sheltered in basements and prayed the words of Psalm 31: 'In you, Lord, I have taken refuge... come quickly to my rescue... save me in your unfailing love' (NIV).

Whatever lies ahead of us, we can know God's saving power, just as David did.

'We are more than conquerors through him who loved us' (Romans 8:37, NIV). Heavenly Father, help me to make level paths for my feet, that I might keep my hope and faith in you. Amen

MICHELE D. MORRISON

The giant of anxiety

'I have told you these things, so that in me you may have peace. In this world you will have trouble. But take heart! I have overcome the world.' (NIV)

Fear focuses on tangible threats or danger, preparing us to fight or fly; anxiety, on the other hand, is an uneasiness that something undefined may pose a problem. The diabolical anxiety giant morphs into an endless variety of forms, from worry over insomnia or health issues, to relationship concerns, job-related demands and so on. Some anxieties take root in us because of past abuse or trauma; others arise from imagined threats, for example an anxiety over becoming an innocent victim in an unjust prison system. Such a giant can tower over all sorts of universal tasks such as filing tax returns or filling in voting forms.

Anxiety giants grow when we feed them with our nervous attention. As they get bigger, our faith in the power and love of God diminishes. I read that anxiety is a red flag alerting us to our disobedience to God's command: 'Do not be afraid.' The trouble with that assessment is that it compounds worry with a sense of guilt over one's apparent faithlessness.

Anxiety is a crippling mental health issue and may need counselling or medical intervention. Telling a believer to stop focusing on the problem and instead focus on God is not always helpful. But it is powerful to remember that trouble in this world is a giant Jesus foresaw and conquered on the cross. Jesus knows we need him to speak peace to our troubled hearts. He offers us a peace that the world cannot give, and he is a gentle teacher.

Paul counsels, 'Be saturated in prayer throughout each day, offering your faith-filled requests before God with overflowing gratitude. Tell him every detail of your life, then God's wonderful peace that transcends human understanding will guard your heart and mind through Jesus Christ' (Philippians 4:6–7, TPT).

Jesus says, 'My peace I give you' (John 14:27). Who do you know who would benefit from a visit from a friend who is willing and ready to share the good news of peace?

MICHELE D. MORRISON

The giant of loneliness

Long ago the Lord said to Israel: 'I have loved you, my people, with an everlasting love. With unfailing love I have drawn you to myself.' (NLT)

Loneliness has stalked humans since the fall. We were created to be social beings. We were made for relationship, both divine and human. The best thing about the garden of Eden was that Adam and Eve shared daily walks with the creator.

Loneliness afflicted many of the people we read about in the Bible: Leah was lonely in her marriage to Jacob (Genesis 29:31–34) and Elijah, believing he was the only prophet left, wanted to die (1 Kings 19). Jesus endured the most intense loneliness, sweating blood as he foresaw that his beloved Father would have to turn his face away from him as he bore our sins on the cross (Luke 22:44).

A quick Google search reveals a number of Christian books addressing loneliness. We saw the problem exacerbated during the Covid-19 lockdowns as people were separated by walls and masks, losing or distorting social interaction. How can we slay this cruel giant that stalks our lives?

First, we must readjust our perspective and remind ourselves that God has loved us, does love us and always will love us. This is our primary relationship, and because God promises again and again in scripture that he will never leave nor forsake us and that he is always with us, we can know that, in fact, we are never alone.

Second, because God made us for relationship, he designed church, where we gather with other believers to love God with all our heart, soul, mind and spirit, and to love others like we love ourselves. I know it doesn't always happen. Sometimes church can be a lonely place, but we need to persevere. If this giant is one that threatens you, maybe try 'church' on a small-group scale. Gather together with a few others, study scripture, eat and laugh and pray together.

'I am with you and will watch over you wherever you go' (Genesis 28:15, NIV). You never abandon any of us, Jesus. Thank you that your presence overshadows the giant of loneliness. Amen

MICHELE D. MORRISON

The giant of depression

The Lord is close to all whose hearts are crushed by pain, and he is always ready to restore the repentant one. (TPT)

Climate change, the pandemic, war in Europe: who hasn't been broken-hearted and crushed in recent years? I believe we all meet the criteria for Jesus to rescue us! But today we are considering those for whom the giant of depression looms into view even when things look rosy.

Recently I heard a man testify that when everything was going well – he was pastor at a successful church, and he and his wife had just had a beautiful baby – he found himself lost in a darkness of spirit he couldn't explain or escape. Winston Churchill called it 'the black dog'.

In the Bible, the prophet Elijah felt so crushed that he prayed to die. 'I have had enough, Lord,' he said, 'Take my life' (1 Kings 19:4, NIV). God didn't take his life, but he did take care of Elijah, sending an angel with food and revealing himself to him.

Similarly, when we face depression, we need friends who will listen to us with compassion and understanding. We need people who will bring meals, walk alongside us or even sit with us in that darkened room – not to try to fix it, just to be with us, praying in the silence.

I'm not sure that depression really fits into this series because clinical depression is a mental health issue which has physiological causes. I wouldn't call cancer or heart disease a Goliath, and nor should I call depression a Goliath. But I think it's valid to include it because, for many who are blissfully unaffected by depression, it can be easy to tell someone to 'buck up' or go for a brisk walk, which can be completely unhelpful.

Depression can be treated with medication or other solutions, but while those treatments are underway, the sufferer's friends, family and church have crucial roles to play in standing with her. Jesus promises his presence, his closeness and a place of refuge in which to recover.

---

*'Come to me, all you who are weary and burdened, and I will give you rest'
(Matthew 11:28, NIV). Lord Jesus, draw near today to those who are crushed
and low in spirit, and give them rest. Amen*

MICHELE D. MORRISON

The giant of temptation

No temptation has overtaken you except what is common to mankind. And God is faithful; he will not let you be tempted beyond what you can bear. (NIV)

There's a good Scottish word to describe the giant of temptation: sleekit. He sits on your shoulder and whispers suggestions into your ear. Some of his temptations are immediately identifiable as contrary to God's ways: sexual immorality and idolatry are mentioned in this passage. But what about the temptation to grumble? How good am I at resisting that giant?

The truth is, not very, especially during challenging times. It is so easy to join in the chorus of gripes, or even to lead it! 'Can you believe what the government is doing now?' 'Why should we put up with…?'

I think it's time I followed a negativity fast. I've done it before, but I seem to have sat down at the table of grumblers again. A negativity fast is a good discipline. It encourages me to be aware of my words and thoughts, and to replace the negative ones with positive words and thoughts based on God's promises.

Grumbling is a sleekit giant never far from my shoulder, but there are many other sneaky giants of temptation. The enemy has identified your vulnerabilities, and you can be sure those are the temptations which will come your way. What might be your weakness: an indulgence in too much red wine or gin; a flutter on the horses to the point of financial disaster; cruel, violent depictions on media screens; gossip?

In *The Message* Bible translation, Eugene Peterson translates this passage: 'We are just as capable of messing it up as they were. Don't be so naive and self-confident. You're not exempt… Cultivate God-confidence.'

Cultivate God-confidence. When we put on the armour of God (Ephesians 6), putting all our trust in him, we can face the giants of temptation and resist them.

'Resist the devil, and he will flee from you' (James 4:7). Lord Jesus Christ, may I be alert to the devil's sly tactics today, ready and willing to resist temptation in your powerful name. Amen

MICHELE D. MORRISON

The giant of despair

When everything was hopeless, Abraham believed anyway, deciding to live not on the basis of what he saw he *couldn't* do but on what God said he *would* do. (MSG)

I am writing this in the second month of Russia's invasion of Ukraine. I pray that by the time this is published, we will be looking back at this moment as a bad dream. Meanwhile, we are still facing the ongoing Covid-19 pandemic and its repercussions. This global crisis has taught me that all I have is this day, this moment. I can't control tomorrow or even imagine what it will bring, but I can control (with God's help) my focus, and as I keep my eyes on him, I am reminded that everything is possible – even peace in Ukraine.

One of the great encouragements I take from this verse in Romans is that the writer focuses on Abraham's eventual victory over hopelessness. The Old Testament chronicles the times that he failed to keep hoping and trusting in God's promises: notably when he lied about Sarai's relationship to him as they sought sanctuary in Egypt (Genesis 12:10–13) and when he agreed with Sarai to take matters into their own hands and use poor, voiceless Hagar to bring about the promised dynasty (Genesis 16:1–2).

I've been there myself, trying to help God bring his promises to fruition through my own clever means. The most obvious of my own personal struggles is the publication of a novel which I believe God commissioned. I believe he promised to bring the publisher, but that hasn't stopped me trying to help him! One day, the book will be published, but I do find it challenging to keep hope alive, waiting on God's timing.

'I can do all this through him who gives me strength' (Philippians 4:13, NIV).
'May the God of hope fill you with all joy and peace… so that you may over-flow with hope by the power of the Holy Spirit' (Romans 15:13, NIV).
MICHELE D. MORRISON

The giant of bitter discontent

Make sure no one gets left out of God's generosity. Keep a sharp eye out for weeds of bitter discontent. A thistle or two gone to seed can ruin a whole garden in no time. (MSG)

A few years ago, my husband Don helped me dig over a couple of flower beds which were riddled with ground elder. This pernicious weed seemed on a mission to conquer the garden. Don dug deeply and thoroughly, and then we replanted; but still, the ground elder appeared, sprouting and spreading as before. It continues its invasion, and I continue digging and pulling and striving to eradicate it.

'See to it… that no bitter root grows up to cause trouble' is how the NIV translates verse 15. However hard you might work at getting rid of a memory of a slight or an affront, it's very easy for one or two details to remain, only to spring to life when something resurrects the memory. When that memory is fed by mental rehearsals of the incident(s), it grows into a grudge, which becomes a giant that can easily block out the light of life.

Self-discipline is called for here. We need to remain on the alert, vigilant for the slightest sign of this giant's reappearance. But self-discipline and self-effort are not enough to slay this giant. It requires partnering with Jesus, who is sensitive to our cries for help in resisting feeding that bitter root. Just like the ground elder in my garden, we need to recognise any new growth of bitterness as soon as it appears, when it is more easily eradicated than when it has grown high, flowered and defiled many.

I am a person who always sidesteps confrontation. When we were first married, I let a lot of things go, until finally that proverbial straw would break the camel's back, and in the ensuing tirade I would trot out all the past weeks' complaints. See to it, scripture says, that you don't do that.

'Be kind and compassionate to one another, forgiving each other, just as in Christ God forgave you' (Ephesians 4:32, NIV). I am still challenged by this giant in various relationships. Are you?

MICHELE D. MORRISON

The giant of fear of poverty

'They all gave out of their wealth; but she, out of her poverty, put in everything – all she had to live on.' (NIV)

We are living through a recession. Here in the UK, there are food shortages and soaring power costs, and many people are living in fear of having to make a choice between having a meal or heating their homes.

I grew up in the baby-boomer generation in California, after the war. I remember the mending basket at the end of the couch. Mom made our clothes and darned our socks. When they were fully worn out, they went into the rag bag in the broom cupboard, to be used for cleaning. We were thrifty.

I love this story of Jesus watching a poor widow give all she had to God. I'm moved by the love he shows her, and I'm challenged by her love for God which freed her to trust him to provide for her every need. That's a goal I'm aiming for in my life. I want to be able to keep my eyes on Jesus, and not on my bank account, for security. Perhaps many of us struggle with this giant, aware that we are called to be responsible stewards of all we are given, and also to be generous.

When speaking to the rich young man (Mark 10:21), Jesus told him to sell everything he had and give it to the poor, and he would have made a deposit of treasure in heaven. Then, Jesus said, follow me.

The rich young man couldn't do it. His wealth shackled him, whereas the widow's poverty set her free. It's not about how much we have, but our attitude to it. Do we live fearfully in the valley shrouded by the shadow of the giant of poverty? How can we slay this giant?

That's exactly what the disciples asked Jesus. And his answer should be our declaration: 'All things are possible with God.'

'With God all things are possible' (Matthew 19:26). Father, give me open-handed generosity coming from a deep inner peace and trust in you to provide for all my needs. Amen

MICHELE D. MORRISON

The giant of addiction

The Lord is my rock, my fortress and my deliverer; my God is my rock, in whom I take refuge, my shield and the horn of my salvation, my stronghold. (NIV)

Jesus rebuked Peter: 'Get behind me, Satan!... you do not have in mind the concerns of God, but merely human concerns' (Matthew 16:23). This illustrates an important principle: recognise your enemy. Giants come in many forms, but Satan is behind each one. He knows our weaknesses and will exploit them mercilessly.

There are all sorts of things that can divert us from the things of God, numbing our minds and enslaving us in worldly pursuits. It may be smoking or substance abuse, immoral behaviour or porn, or perhaps trash TV or an electronic device. Addiction to digital devices may be the most insidious and harmful crutch of all, dragging old and young into its vicious web. It isn't just the negative self-image that might result and spawn suicidal thoughts and sometimes actions. It's the wedge it creates in relationships.

I was once in a restaurant with my mother and my daughter. As I crossed the dining area to go and use the bathroom, I noticed that people at every table were on their phones, scrolling through social media. The message conveyed is that whatever is available on this little hand-held device is of more import and interest than the person sitting in front of them. They were more attentive to the words and images of a stranger on the web than to those of their companion.

James wrote in his letter, 'Resist the devil, and he will flee from you' (James 4:7). We do not need to fear the giant of addiction, but we do need to recognise him, and then we can resist.

'In all these things we are more than conquerors through him who loved us' (Romans 8:37). Whenever I am tempted by an addiction, help me, Lord, to address the real enemy as you did: Get behind me, Satan! Amen

MICHELE D. MORRISON

The giant of poor self-image

'I have loved you with an everlasting love; I have drawn you with unfailing kindness.' (NIV)

What influences your perception of yourself: the mirror on the wall, comments on Facebook or Instagram, historic criticism, friends or family? Poor self-image results from believing the withering giant of others' assessments of our looks or abilities, rather than trusting in the truth of holy scripture. 'Before I formed you in the womb,' God says, 'I knew you' (Jeremiah 1:5).

The world likes to tell us that we are not enough. 'Perfect' faces and bodies on the internet or other media outlets infer that we don't measure up. The unaccountability of social media comments encourages people to belittle and mock one another. Sensitive – and even not-so-sensitive – souls can be diminished and devastated by vicious remarks made by others.

There has been a huge increase in mental health issues, particularly among teenage girls. These include eating disorders, where (mainly) young women often perceive distorted images of themselves in the mirror, seen through the lens of photoshopped images they see in the media.

Poor self-image undermines our confidence and hinders our efforts to step boldly into the calling God has on our lives. If this is an issue for you, make the words spoken in Joshua 1:9 your own, and speak them out loud every time you falter: 'I am not afraid or discouraged, for the Lord my God is with me wherever I go.'

The Lord helped me to overcome a self-image of inadequacy in public speaking, but still that bogeyman rears its head from time to time. Nudged to run a Lenten series on the persecuted church, my confidence faltered until I was given a word from God: 'Rise up... take courage and do it' (Ezra 10:4). The meetings blessed the dozen or so who attended, and who knows the ripple effect on the persecuted church.

God loves me with an everlasting love. John 3:16 tells me that God loved me so much, he gave his only, much-loved Son to die for me, so that I might live with him forever.

MICHELE D. MORRISON

The giant of global threats

'And who knows but that you have come to your royal position for such a time as this?' (NIV)

Such a time as this. Have you ever known such a time as this? There is a global pandemic, killing millions and still mutating and moving throughout the world; a climate emergency that threatens the extinction of so much of what makes up our planet's biodiversity; the fall of Kabul and ensuing carnage and chaos; if all this weren't enough, President Putin decided to invade Ukraine.

Such a time as this. The perfect storm. Hopefully, by the time you are reading this, things will have moved on: Covid-19 will have joined the array of other viruses which cause us discomfort but rarely kill; we will be making real progress in reaching zero carbon emissions and living less wasteful and more responsible lives; the Taliban will no longer rule in Afghanistan; and the war in Ukraine will have resolved and peace and reconstruction will have ensued.

But there is a possibility that other crises will have arisen to take their place. Is it any wonder that so many of us are paralysed by the giant of global threats? How do we live in peace during times of tumult?

The refrain of this fortnight is to 'turn our eyes upon Jesus'. He is the giant-slayer. We look to him for deliverance, not in desperation but in trust that he will keep his promises. He is with us in everything.

When there was serious talk of a nuclear threat from Russia, I was asked how I could sleep at night. I replied that we all will die at some time or another, and because I am confident that the next world is infinitely better than this one, I am not afraid. The Lord will take me home when my time is up. My fearful questioner was immediately reassured.

'What is seen is temporary, but what is unseen is eternal' (2 Corinthians 4:18). Our present troubles produce for us a glory that vastly outweighs them and will last forever!

MICHELE D. MORRISON

The giant of pride

'This is what the Lord says: Do not be afraid! Don't be discouraged by this mighty army, for the battle is not yours, but God's.' (NLT)

There has been a recurring theme throughout this study, urging us all to recognise our dependence on God and learn to rely on him. What hinders that willingness to rely on God? Could it be the giant of pride?

My parents used to laugh lovingly as they recounted my antics as a growing toddler. If they tried to help me with something, I would declare forcefully, 'I can do it myself!' What might be cute in the mouth of a young child loses its sparkle in the mouths of arrogant adults. Until we recognise that we can't do everything ourselves, we will often fall prey to a cohort of giants.

Years ago, my husband Don and I wrote a puppet show illustrating this passage, in which the recurring line was, 'Lord, we don't know what to do, but Lord, our eyes are on you!' I am grateful for that exercise because that line is well and truly embedded in my mind and spirit, and I often repeat it when under pressure.

Our culture encourages us to make our own assessments of what is right and wrong. It's become a tenet of political correctness that what's right for you might not be right for me, and vice versa. This thinking threatens society itself: we are designed to live in community and in relationship, which requires cooperation in agreeing a common vision of truth and a sharing of values. Society is breaking on the rocks of pride.

Rather than being stridently independent, let's be people of humility, worshiping the almighty God. As we praise, we shall rise up in joyful relief that the battle is indeed the Lord's.

Say 'No' to the giant of pride and 'Yes' to humility, 'Yes' to trust in God and 'Yes' to the truth as revealed in Jesus Christ.

'At the very moment [the singers] began to sing and give praise, the Lord caused the armies of [the enemies] to start fighting among themselves' (2 Chronicles 20:22). *Give thanks to the Lord, sing and praise him.*

MICHELE D. MORRISON

The story of Noah

Jackie Harris writes:

I encountered two stumbling blocks as I began to study the story of Noah. First, I had to put aside images from children's Bibles and story books of cute animals lining up two by two to enter the ark. This is quite a sombre tale. It's the story of a man, living out his faith in a totally immoral and corrupt society, who is called to do something extraordinary. It's a story of judgement and devastation, but also of promise and restoration.

Second, I had to avoid getting side-tracked by discussions about its authenticity. Is it fact or fable? Was there really a flood that covered the whole earth? How does the biblical account fit in with what scientists and historians have discovered about the ancient world? This can be very interesting, but not particularly life changing.

One of the most helpful things I read said that the purpose of these early chapters of Genesis is to teach us about God and humanity. When I focused on that, I discovered this well-known tale has much to teach us about faith, perseverance, trust and God's grace, and we will be exploring these themes in the days ahead.

I have arranged the daily readings to take us through the whole narrative in Genesis 6—9, but my notes sometimes go back and forth and focus on selected passages. If you have time, it would be a good idea to read through the whole story in one sitting before we begin.

As you read, you might wonder what we could possibly have in common with Noah. I'd like to suggest two things to start us off. First, the description of the society in which Noah lived – 'corrupt… full of violence' (Genesis 6:11, NIV) – sounds all too familiar. Certainly, stories of violence and corruption seem to dominate the headlines. Noah may have lived thousands of years ago, but his world sounds very like ours.

Second, this is a man who experienced a great deal of upheaval. He was a farmer who became a builder, a conservationist, a pioneer and then a farmer again. He knew what it was to live in a bustling neighbourhood, a confined space and the freedom of open country. He had to be adaptable and open to change – two things increasingly demanded of us in our fast-paced world.

So, let's unpack his story and see what we can learn from this remarkable man and his relationship with God.

Living faithfully

Noah was a righteous man, blameless among the people of his time, and he walked faithfully with God. (NIV)

I must admit I am in awe of this description of Noah. He was righteous at a time when everyone else was seemingly turning their backs on God. The world in which Noah lived was marred by corruption and violence (v. 11); so much so that God was regretting that he made human beings. Noah, though, was different; he stood out. It occurs to me that this is not always a comfortable place to be. It takes courage not to run with the pack.

But it is that little phrase 'he walked faithfully with God' (v. 9) that I have been mulling over. It speaks of a close relationship, of a man who consistently sought to follow God's will and to honour his ways. Interestingly, it is exactly the same phrase that is used to describe Enoch, Noah's great-grandfather (5:24). Enoch enjoyed such close fellowship with God that one day God simply took him home. Perhaps Noah had the benefit of a godly heritage, of faith and knowledge of God passed down through the generations. Did this help him to stand out from the crowd?

Having a godly family is a real blessing, but faith has to be personal. Another little phrase caught my eye: 'Noah found favour in the eyes of the Lord' (v. 8). It was Noah's own conduct, his own willingness to live differently from those around him and to follow God's ways that caught God's attention.

I am reminded of the words of the psalmist: 'Blessed is the one who does not walk in step with the wicked... but whose delight is in the law of the Lord' (Psalm 1:1–2). That's Noah – a righteous man who walks faithfully with God.

Like Noah, we have a choice to make. Will we follow God's ways in our generation or simply go with the flow? Pray for the courage to live differently.

JACKIE HARRIS

Trustworthy and trusting

Make yourself an ark of cypress wood … You are to bring into the ark two of all living creatures, male and female, to keep them alive with you … And Noah did all that the Lord commanded him. (NIV)

Trust is at the heart of this story. My dictionary defines trust as 'a firm belief in the truth, reliability, or ability of someone or something'. Amazingly we see not only Noah's trust in God, but also God's trust in Noah. God trusts Noah enough to take him into his confidence and ultimately to ensure the survival of all that he has created. His plans for the restoration of his creation rest in this one man. And Noah trusts God. His response is simply to do 'everything just as God commanded him' (6:22). He trusts God enough to take on this extraordinary commission.

I'm struck by the specific and detailed instructions Noah is given in order to prepare for the coming disaster, but also by the enormity of the task. This is a long-term commitment. It is going to require great care, meticulous attention to detail, a phenomenal amount of hard work and presumably great cost. And what about other people's reactions? What did the neighbours think as he put all his energy into building the ark and warned of a coming disaster? Did they ridicule him or simply ignore him?

Whatever the difficulties, Noah takes God at his word, follows his instructions to the letter and trusts God for the outcome. No wonder Noah is mentioned in the great chapter on faith in Hebrews 11!

I don't know what challenges me the most: Noah's complete trust and obedience in the face of such a huge undertaking and possible public criticism or his trustworthiness – the fact that God saw in him someone he could count on to do his will. What about you?

'Trust in the Lord with all your heart and lean not on your own understanding; in all your ways submit to him, and he will make your paths straight' (Proverbs 3:5–6).

JACKIE HARRIS

Safe in God's care

On that very day Noah and his sons, Shem, Ham and Japheth, together with his wife and the wives of his three sons, entered the ark… Then the Lord shut him in. (NIV)

The details of the flood are devastating. Literally every living thing is wiped out (v. 23). Notice that not only do the floodgates of the heaves open, but also 'the springs of the great deep burst forth' (v. 11). This description is reminiscent of the creation story in Genesis 1 where God separates the waters (Genesis 1:6–7). It is as if God is undoing his creation. The rain falls, the waters rise and everything is gone. Only Noah and those in the ark with him are left.

Amid all the destruction, there is one small detail I want to focus on. It is God himself who closes the door of the ark once everyone is inside (v. 16). We saw yesterday how God gave very detailed instructions about how to build the ark and who should go in. Now, at the very brink of judgement, God wants to ensure that everyone is accounted for and secure in the place of safety he designed.

One day God will restore the earth again and, just as in the time of Noah, there is a place of safety for all those who trust him – not in an ark, but through a relationship with Jesus. Jesus is the 'gate' through which we enter to be saved (John 10:7–10).

We thought yesterday of what it cost Noah to build the ark. Perhaps we could spend some time today thinking about what it cost God to enable us to be safe in his care both now and forevermore. 'For God so loved the world that he gave his one and only Son, that whoever believes in him shall not perish but have eternal life' (John 3:16).

Father God, as I remind myself of what you have done for me, may I trust more and more in your love and care. Thank you for making it possible for me to have eternal life with you. Amen

JACKIE HARRIS

Waiting in faith

After forty days Noah opened a window… and sent out a raven… Then he sent out a dove… But the dove could find nowhere to perch… so it returned to Noah… He waited seven more days and again sent out the dove. (NIV)

Waiting appears to be a significant theme in Noah's story. Perhaps I notice that because I don't find waiting easy. I am usually either frustrated or anxious, sometimes both, but there's no sense of that here.

First, there's a period of 100 years between God telling Noah to build the ark and him actually going in. And in all that time, 'Noah did all that the Lord commanded him' (7:5). In other words, in this long period of waiting for God to act, Noah simply gets on with the job he's been given.

Then, Noah and his family must wait out the storm inside the ark. Outside, the rains fall and the seas rise, but inside the ark must have been busy too. Life would be very different to what it had been before. There would be new routines and ways of doing things; adjustments would be made as they shared a confined space. It was a place of safety, but perhaps not always of comfort.

Finally, we see Noah waiting in hope as the rain ceases and the waters begin to recede. Noah tests the situation by sending out a raven at first and then a dove, and then waits for God's direction. The earth is looking increasingly dry (vv. 13–14), but Noah waits patiently for God's time and his instruction to leave (v. 15).

I wonder if any of these waiting times resonate with you? Is God calling you to be obedient and simply get on with the job in hand, to trust in his care amid changing circumstances or to seek his way forward and wait patiently for direction? Does it help to realise that waiting often involves action of some sort?

Father, waiting is hard. Help me to discern what you want me to do in these circumstances, to trust in your timing and to recognise your care and provision for me. Amen

JACKIE HARRIS

Making a fresh start

Then Noah built an altar to the Lord and, taking some of the clean animals and clean birds, he sacrificed burnt offerings on it. (NIV)

New beginnings can be exciting – a new job, a new home, a new ministry or perhaps a new season of life. We start with a clean slate and high hopes of how things might develop; but new beginnings can also be a little daunting – things will be different, and we don't want to make any mistakes or get off on the wrong foot. I think we can learn a lot from Noah about new beginnings.

We saw yesterday how Noah patiently waited for God to tell him when it was right to leave the ark. What a relief it must have been to step out on to firm ground again, to feel the sun and smell the air. I think if I had been cooped up for a long time in the ark, the first thing I would want to do is to run around and explore my new surroundings, maybe start making plans for a home and how to cultivate the land again. Not Noah. Noah's first act is to give thanks, to make an offering and to seek God's blessing for the future. This was a new beginning and Noah wanted to do things right.

When God gives us something new, let's think creatively about how we might give thanks and make an offering. For example, a new home might encourage us to offer a gift to support the homeless; a new job might inspire us to make a commitment to pray for our colleagues.

Perhaps you are thinking that there is no opportunity for a fresh start at the moment. Someone once told me that we have the opportunity to make a fresh start with God every day. That's certainly something to be thankful for and who knows where that might lead?

Father, thank you that there are always new opportunities with you. Grant me a fresh start with you today and help me to see how I might express my gratitude for your goodness. Amen

JACKIE HARRIS

God's kindness revealed

Then God said to Noah and to his sons with him: 'I now establish my covenant with you and with your descendants after you and with every living creature that was with you.' (NIV)

Today, we focus on God's covenant with Noah. It is the first covenant God makes with humankind. When a covenant was made in the ancient world, it signified a relationship based on commitment. Promises were made, conditions were set down and there were consequences if the obligations were not met. This covenant however is unique.

First, it is inclusive. The covenant was first alluded to before the flood (6:8), although it was directed solely to Noah. Now it embraces the whole family: his sons, his wife, his daughters-in-law and indeed the whole of creation are the recipients of God's promise. It's a promise for everyone.

Second, it is unconditional. Nothing is required of Noah and his family or their descendants. This covenant is based on God's faithfulness alone. Despite knowing that humankind will continue to turn away from him (8:21), God will keep his word.

Third, this covenant is permanent. It is 'for all generations to come' (v. 12). We too are recipients of God's promise that seedtime and harvest, summer and winter, day and night will continue as long as the earth endures (8:22).

Finally, God seals his covenant with a sign – the rainbow – to give reassurance. We have God's assurance that when a rainbow is seen, God will remember his promise.

This covenant reveals God's kindness, but it is nothing to the kindness we have received. The apostle Paul sums it up beautifully: 'But when the kindness and love of God our Saviour appeared, he saved us, not because of righteous things we had done, but because of his mercy. He saved us through the washing of rebirth and renewal by the Holy Spirit, whom he poured out on us generously through Jesus Christ our Saviour' (Titus 3:4–6). How gracious is our God!

In Titus 3:8, Paul urges people to respond to God's kindness by devoting themselves to doing good. What might this look like for you in the coming days?
                                                              JACKIE HARRIS

An unhappy ending

Noah, a man of the soil, proceeded to plant a vineyard. When he drank some of its wine, he became drunk and lay uncovered inside his tent. (NIV)

After the drama of the flood, the joy of life beginning again and receiving God's promises and blessings, life seemingly quietens down for Noah and his family. Noah returns to being a farmer and plants a vineyard. Unfortunately, he gets drunk on the wine he produces.

There is no comment made about Noah's drunkenness; rather, the focus is on how his sons respond. His youngest, Ham, makes fun of his father and clearly hopes his brothers will join in. However, Shem and Japheth seek to respect their father and act honourably. Their actions were to have far-reaching consequences for their descendants. So, what do we make of this rather ignominious ending to the story of Noah and his family?

I think there are two main lessons we can draw.

First, like Shem and Japheth, we need to ensure we respect our parents, even if they behave unwisely. 'Honour your father and your mother' is one of the ten commandments God gave his people (Exodus 20:12), so clearly this is important. We might want to broaden this and think about how we treat people generally. Do we take advantage of people who make poor decisions or join in making fun of others?

Second, we need to be wary when life becomes settled and routine. Noah had always enjoyed a close walk with God, but now we see him behaving unwisely. However, it's what the story doesn't say that made me think. It doesn't say, 'Noah walked with God another 350 years and then he died', but only that he lived another 350 years (v. 28). Perhaps I'm reading too much into that, but let's be careful and ensure we are walking with God not just through the ups and downs, but through all the ordinary bits of life in between.

Father, help me to stay close to you in every circumstance, not just when life is challenging, and grant me wisdom in the way I behave and in the way I treat others. I want my story to end well. Amen

JACKIE HARRIS

Wisdom for life

Sheila Jacobs writes:

It's quite a long time since I looked through the Old Testament treasure of Proverbs. However, while reading Proverbs as I was preparing to write these notes, I was struck by the amount of down-to-earth advice that can be found here.

The main author (although there are others too) is King Solomon – a bit of a giveaway is found in 1:1 (NIV) – 'The proverbs of Solomon son of David, king of Israel'. In 1 Kings 3, we read of Solomon's humility in asking God for discernment in ruling God's people and of God graciously granting him 'a wise and discerning heart' (1 Kings 3:12, NIV). How sad, then, that such a wise man should finish his life poorly, led astray by his wives, as we read in 1 Kings 11:3.

The purpose of Proverbs can be found in the prologue in chapter 1. The writer wants us to be instructed by the insight to be found here, so that we can live well, and do 'what is right and just and fair' (v. 3, NIV). Through these teachings we can learn to be discerning and find guidance for our lives. Proverbs is essentially a manual for life and is as relevant to us now as it was in the days of Solomon. It instructs us about relationships, work, wealth and how to live well alongside our friends, family and community, and it exhorts us to find wisdom and avoid folly. It is interesting to note that both Wisdom and Folly, personified throughout Proverbs, are depicted as female!

The proverbs of Solomon are contained in chapters 10 to 22:16 and chapters 25 to 29. In between are 30 sayings of the wise, then the book ends with wisdom from Agur and King Lemuel and an epilogue about the wife of noble character.

We are going to dart about in Proverbs, so I hope you will bear with me. We'll look at themes and draw points from them, but it won't be possible to look at the whole book in just 14 days. I will leave that to you, but I commend reading it over a period of weeks, just a few verses at a time – see how God uses it to speak to you, enhance your life, bless and challenge you.

I pray that you will find these notes both interesting and thought-provoking!

The fear of the Lord

The fear of the Lord is the beginning of wisdom, and knowledge of the Holy One is understanding. For through wisdom your days will be many, and years will be added to your life. (NIV)

In Proverbs 1:7, there is a similar exhortation: 'The fear of the Lord is the beginning of knowledge' – it's clear the writer wants us to know just how important the fear of God is, and it's a great way to begin these notes.

What is 'the fear of the Lord'? And how is it the beginning of wisdom and understanding? It could be that you don't remember a time when you were not a Christian. You may have loved Jesus all your life. However, I can certainly recall a time when I didn't know him, even though I may have called myself a Christian! It was only when I hit a period of turbulence and called out to God, experiencing his peace, that I really knew that Jesus was alive. That encounter turned my world upside down.

I knew I had to find a church – churchgoing wasn't something that I normally did. I went to a local fellowship and felt the presence of God in such power that I was quite shaken. I went home thinking, 'It's all true'. I was awed by the compelling sense of God's presence I had experienced. God was real. He was 'other than me'. He was powerful.

I'm not sure I got much sleep that night. I remember staring into the darkness for ages, overwhelmed. When I went to work the next day, I recall looking at my colleagues, thinking, 'Life is being lived on a different level and you just don't realise it.'

The Lord is great and awesome. Yet I come to God as my Father because Jesus made it possible for me to approach him. Jesus died and rose from the dead so I could know God.

I hope I never take this amazing privilege for granted!

Are you ever tempted to take your relationship with God for granted?

SHEILA JACOBS

Leaning on him

Trust in the Lord with all your heart and lean not on your own understanding; in all your ways submit to him, and he will make your paths straight. (NIV)

Along with a healthy reverence for God, we need to trust him, and we can only trust someone we know. It's when we have known people, usually over a long period of time, and have come to experience their faithfulness to us, that we find we can really trust them. It's hard to trust someone you have only just met – unless they have a solid reputation for integrity.

In John 10, Jesus talks about the importance of knowing his voice (v. 4). As we spend time with him and learn to discern his presence, then we can know what he is saying when we are faced with a path that we are not sure is quite as 'straight' as we might have hoped. To submit to God in all our ways seems like a big ask, doesn't it? What does it mean for me to submit to him my relationships, my job, my income, my health, my future? What if I don't understand what's happening? Can I still trust God and submit to him in the 'I don't knows' of life?

My mother had dementia. She was in a care home for more than 13 years, gradually declining. It was so sad to see. In this, I had to trust God wholeheartedly, not leaning on my own understanding. While I may not have chosen to walk this path – and neither, of course, did my mother – the fact was, as I leaned on God and surrendered the situation to him (often daily), I found that I wasn't walking alone.

My mother frequently spoke about how she felt the presence of God and his joy, even in the middle of her suffering. We need to lean on him – even when we don't 'get it'.

Is there an area of your life where you need to 'lean on him' today?

SHEILA JACOBS

Guard your heart

Above all else, guard your heart, for everything you do flows from it… Give careful thought to the paths for your feet and be steadfast in all your ways. (NIV)

How well do you guard your heart? I must admit I haven't always been very wise in this area. Proverbs 4:5 tells us to 'get wisdom, get understanding' and that's something I know I need!

I have some good friends, who I am very happy to have speak into my life, to counsel me and to give me their advice. I trust them to speak because I know that they care about me. They won't flatter me, they'll tell me the truth – but always in love, as it says in Ephesians 4:15. I like being around my friends. They are a mixed bunch with different personalities. Some are calm, some are fiery, but all are unique and special.

But there is one sort of person who is difficult to befriend. Proverbs 26:21 says, 'As charcoal to embers and as wood to fire, so is a quarrelsome person for kindling strife.' It's just not easy being around someone who is argumentative, is it? It can be very wearying. Perhaps there are people in your life who you find tricky – talking with them can be like walking on eggshells! Or worse – perhaps *we* are the person that people find difficult; maybe they are careful what they say to *us* in case we fly off the handle!

We need to 'give careful thought' to those we choose to spend time with as close friends and confidants because their behaviour will certainly affect our own.

Guarding our hearts can be especially important when it comes to choosing a marriage partner, if that's what we feel God is leading us towards. We need to be careful with our hearts because what happens there will influence our decisions, our behaviour – our lives.

Are you guarding your heart? What's flowing from it today?

SHEILA JACOBS

Conflict

There are six things the Lord hates, seven that are detestable to him... a false witness who pours out lies and a person who stirs up conflict in the community. (NIV)

In this passage we discover some of the Lord's pet hates, which include a false witness and people who 'stir up conflict' (v. 19).

Unity within the Christian community is so important. Jesus said: 'As I have loved you, so you must love one another. By this everyone will know that you are my disciples, if you love one another' (John 13:34–35). So, our greatest witness to a world lost in sin is to love each other – love other Christians.

Now, this isn't always easy to do, as I'm sure you realise! There are some people we gravitate to and get along with more naturally. But how do we build good relationships with others, especially those who may have different doctrinal views than us? Is it okay to disagree, and to just leave it at that?

I think 'stirring up conflict' is to deliberately set out to pick an argument with someone. It's like me sitting in a café, knowing the people at the next table think differently on a topic, and loudly proclaiming my own view, just to get their blood boiling. It's provoking them. It's trying to pick a fight. It can also be done in an underhand way, by dropping little words of criticism into the ear of a third party. Sometimes it is wise not to involve people in our own spats and disputes, trusting instead a good friend or Christian leader who will listen to us and pray, rather than take sides and become embroiled in what is essentially someone else's issue.

Creating division between people is not how God wants us to live – especially when this involves his own children. Let's try to live at peace and agree to disagree. Scoring points always tends to backfire.

Is there an area of conflict known to you, that is creating division in your family or your church? Ask God to bring peace to that problem.

SHEILA JACOBS

Gossip

Whoever derides their neighbour has no sense, but the one who has understanding holds their tongue. A gossip betrays a confidence, but a trustworthy person keeps a secret. (NIV)

Proverbs has a lot to say about how we speak to others and what we say. Here we're warned against gossip. Have you ever trusted someone with a secret, only to find that it has been broadcast – and perhaps come back to you with a bit of embellishment? It can be devastating when it is something that is profoundly sensitive. Some friendships never recover from the effects of gossip.

Proverbs 10:19 tells us that 'the prudent hold their tongues' and Proverbs 17:27 suggests that those who have knowledge use their words 'with restraint'.

I remember hearing the expression, 'Hold your tongue!' many years ago. I have often spoken and wished I hadn't (just as I have also not spoken at times and wished I had). We must be very prudent, as Proverbs suggests, when it comes to talking.

You might be the kind of person who loves talking; you like communicating and enjoy a good chat with your friends and family. Unfortunately, we can often become too garrulous, and that can lead to problems. 'Oops, shouldn't have told you that.' 'Sorry, I think she told me not to say anything. Keep it to yourself, will you?' 'I don't want to gossip, but did you know…' Or perhaps the one many of us are guilty of: 'Can you pray for so-and-so? I hear she's in a bit of a pickle. This is what happened…' Hopefully we don't 'deride our neighbour', but I wonder if we ever find ourselves having a bit of a laugh at their expense?

I've spent many years learning how to really listen, and I have many more lessons to learn in this area. Listening and then keeping a confidence is precious; as is speaking well of others, and with understanding.

How good are you at holding your tongue? On a scale of one to ten, how well do you listen?

SHEILA JACOBS

Friends

One who has unreliable friends soon comes to ruin, but there is a friend who sticks closer than a brother. (NIV)

Today's passage starts out with an exhortation to run to God, who is a 'fortified tower' where we can find safety, and ends with the text above. In between are various proverbs, including 'the tongue has the power of life and death' (v. 21).

Perhaps you can remember words that were spoken over you, even as a child. Maybe they weren't great – 'You're no good', 'You'll never succeed' – or perhaps they were affirming – 'You did that well', 'You look lovely'. Yet it is often the negative words that strike deeply, so much so that our sense of self-esteem, our value, our worth, our self-confidence or even our talent can seem to die a little.

Proverbs has so much to say about how we speak, as we saw in yesterday's note. How we speak and what we say can have a huge effect not just on others but also on ourselves. What's your own self-talk like?

The 'unreliable friends' mentioned above are people we can't trust. Indeed, they may not only prove unreliable, but they might also inflict more damage than we know. Are your friends the kind of people who support and encourage you, or do they criticise and belittle you?

We all fail in many ways. We let others down, in thought, word and deed, and they let us down too. We are all human. We also let God down. Happily, he is still the 'fortified tower' (v. 10) who is unchanging. We can always run to him when we are alone, frightened or feel a long way from him. His invitation is always there. He is the friend who will stick closer than any relative – mother, father, sister, brother – or even the closest companion.

Lord, you are the one who never fails me. You will never let me down. You love me. You are my true friend. Thank you, Jesus. Amen

SHEILA JACOBS

Children

Start children off on the way they should go, and even when they are old they will not turn from it. (NIV)

How difficult it is to watch your child go 'off the rails'. You've brought them up in the ways of God, they've been going to church with you, then all of a sudden, they're not interested.

I only remember going to church a couple of times as a child, apart from when we had to go with school. But I heard a lot about Jesus from my granny. Then, in my late teens I got into the pub and club scene. I remember my granny telling me to 'come out from among them' (see 2 Corinthians 6:17) and thinking, 'I don't want to!' She challenged me when I called myself a Christian and I was annoyed. 'Of course, I'm a Christian!' I retorted.

When everything went wrong, I remembered Grandma's words about Jesus. I'd also read a book that indicated that he was real and could be encountered. I called out to him – and found him.

The point is, I'd gone away from the truth of what I'd been told when I was a child, but then I found Jesus for myself.

Starting children off in the right way lays a good and solid foundation. Hopefully, when they are older, even if they seem to have gone away, they will remember the training of their younger days. As we get older, we tend to reflect more on the past; there can be a sense of returning to our roots.

If you're worried about a young person in your family, pray for them. Thank God for them. Quote today's verse over their life. And if you are bringing up children right now and you're concerned about their future, remember how precious they are to God. Start them off with Jesus.

Father, I thank you for [name the child/young person]. I ask you to watch over them, to keep them safe and to help them walk with you. For your glory, Lord. Amen

SHEILA JACOBS

Covering love

Whoever would foster love covers over an offence, but whoever repeats the matter separates close friends. A rebuke impresses a discerning person. (NIV)

As we have seen, the book of Proverbs has much to say about relationships. Here, we are told to 'cover over an offence' (v. 9) if we want to foster love. Does that mean we just let injustice go? Not at all.

Love sometimes means having that difficult conversation and speaking truth to someone who has offended us. This is better than internalising it, pretending everything is okay and secretly resenting that person – or complaining about it to someone else, without speaking to the person concerned. Such poison can destroy a relationship, but it also does *us* no good.

Forgiveness, and acting in love, can be a tough call. And it may not always be possible to talk with the one who has hurt us. We see the wisdom in not seeking revenge – Proverbs 20:22 tells us we should avoid saying, 'I'll pay you back for this wrong!' and instead wait for the Lord to deal with the situation.

However, there are times when it is entirely appropriate to call out, in love, the one who has offended us. When we do that, it can facilitate a space for reconciliation and forgiveness. Proverbs 10:12 tells us that 'love covers over all wrongs', which is echoed in 1 Peter 4:8: 'Above all, love each other deeply, because love covers over a multitude of sins.' This is what Jesus did for us when he died on the cross and paid the price for our wrongdoing; because of his sacrifice, we are forgiven and able to be in a relationship with God, knowing his love and care.

Forgiving doesn't necessarily mean full restoration of a relationship that may be, for example, abusive in some sense. But covering an offence, even though we may need to address it privately, is acting in love.

Is there someone you are finding it difficult to forgive? Bring this to the Lord. Is it appropriate to speak to them about it? If not, how can you cover over it in love?

SHEILA JACOBS

Wealth

Cast but a glance at riches, and they are gone, for they will surely sprout wings and fly off to the sky like an eagle. (NIV)

I love the picture in these verses of riches sprouting wings. I think many of us will agree that with the price of everything going up, our cash doesn't go as far as it used to! I think there is a difference, though, between working hard – which Proverbs advocates (see for example 14:23) – and making possessions or the pursuit of money our goal in life. Money makes a good servant, but a poor master, to paraphrase Francis Bacon.

The New Testament tells us that the 'love of money is a root of all kinds of evil' (1 Timothy 6:10). Loving it is very different from using it for our own needs and for the benefit of others.

Jesus had much to say about wealth – see for example his dealings with the rich young ruler in Mark 10:17–31. The fact is, the pursuit of money and riches, like anything that gets in the way of our relationship with God, can become an idol if it becomes our main focus in life. In the sermon on the mount, Jesus spoke about perspectives when he talked about choosing to put the kingdom of God first; after all, everything else is transient (Matthew 6:25–34).

I used to be involved in street evangelism in a large town on Saturday nights. I met people who had 'had it all' but lost everything and were living in shop doorways.

Whatever we hanker after in this life, be it that amazing new wardrobe or fantastic smartphone, we need to remember that it will be 'old news' tomorrow. The shiny new car in the driveway will one day need replacing.

Let's make sure that we set our sights right: making Jesus our first priority and re-evaluating everything else in the light of that.

Do you need to rethink your priorities – especially around the pursuit of 'riches', whatever those riches are for you?

SHEILA JACOBS

The poor

Whoever is kind to the poor lends to the Lord, and he will reward them for what they have done. (NIV)

These wise words – and the flipside, 'Whoever oppresses the poor shows contempt for their Maker, but whoever is kind to the needy honours God' (14:31) – another important point in the book of Proverbs. Yesterday we looked at perspectives when it comes to wealth, today we're thinking about what we might do with our money.

It's not a bad thing to have wealth. The problem is focusing on it to the extent that everything else fades into the background. When we have money and material goods, we are blessed; and that blessing can be used to help others.

In Matthew 6:3, Jesus tells us that giving to the needy is something that should really be done in secret. We don't need to go around showing off how much good we do. God sees what is done, and that is enough; he will reward those who do these things (Matthew 6:4).

The book of Proverbs talks lots about the poor – in chapter 28 it says 'a ruler who oppresses the poor is like driving rain that leaves no crops' (v. 3), which is pretty descriptive. Rich and poor have one thing in common. The Lord is 'the Maker' of both (22:2). What a great leveller this is.

Sometimes we may find ourselves judging people who are living in difficult circumstances. We may even blame them for making poor choices; but life happens. When I was ill in my 30s, I spent years unable to work. God graciously restored my health and ability to earn, but it was a humbling time.

There are so many places of need in this world. I wonder how God is moving your heart to help and bless those who have little or nothing.

Is there any cause known to you that you have been thinking about supporting for a while, and perhaps never got around to? Is now the time to help out in some way?

SHEILA JACOBS

Skills and talents

Do you see someone skilled in their work? They will serve before kings; they will not serve before officials of low rank. (NIV)

One of the things I've noticed when I have been studying these passages in Proverbs is how the writer advocates working rather than 'chasing fantasies' (28:19; see also 12:11). Hard work brings a reward (12:14), profit (14:23) and praise (31:31).

There are many reasons why we may not all have paid work: through retirement, ill health, unemployment or other life situations such as looking after children. Maybe we delight, though, in a craft, skill or hobby. Perhaps our area of excellence is in relationships – in simply listening to others or helping them in some way.

We probably all know people who have spent their lives chasing fantasies. Maybe they are people who queue up for a lottery ticket, hoping their lives will change forever as they trust in luck.

Do we want change? Maybe the Lord is asking us to do something!

When we enjoy a task, we want to do it well. And when we do it well, it can bring us a sense of satisfaction, and often blesses other people.

Is there something you have longed to do, but have never had the courage or opportunity to start? Perhaps you have dreamt about writing a novel, riding a horse, learning a musical instrument or taking cookery classes; maybe you have always wanted to go to university, become involved in youth work, get ordained or change careers.

What is it that you feel the Lord has called you to do – what areas has he asked you to excel in? Which skills do you need to hone? Colossians 3:23 tells us: 'Whatever you do, work at it with all your heart, as working for the Lord, not for human masters.' So, what is it God has called you to 'work at with all your heart'?

Lord, I want to be in your will; I want to be in step with the plans you have for my life. Please show me what you want me to do and help me to do it well. Amen

SHEILA JACOBS

Integrity

Whoever walks in integrity walks securely, but whoever takes crooked paths will be found out… The mouth of the righteous is a fountain of life. (NIV)

What does 'to walk in integrity' mean to you? Do those who don't walk righteously always get found out? We all have secret sins, surely? Sometimes these can stay hidden – can't they? – the wrong thought, the selfish action.

God sees our heart (1 Samuel 16:7), and the Holy Spirit gently reminds us of how Jesus wants us to live (John 14:26). Staying in step with him leads to life with real integrity.

However, we all stumble and fall at times. Even with the best will in the world, we are human, and we will, inevitably, get it wrong on occasions. What I think the writer of Proverbs is saying here is that when we consistently take 'crooked paths' our life will be seen for what it is – eventually – even if we try to hide it, perhaps behind good works or religious duties.

Galatians 5:22–23 tells us about the fruit of the Spirit: if he is indwelling us, then we should see the outworking of this fruit more and more, as we walk with him. If this isn't happening, if we are walking in 'crooked paths' even though we know the Holy Spirit is calling us to be different, we need to listen to him, and obey. Sometimes a friend speaking truth into our life can be difficult to hear. But 'the mouth of the righteous', especially when we are being challenged about behaviour, words or lifestyle, can ultimately be a blessing. When we choose to walk God's way, we are choosing to walk securely, knowing we are fulfilling the destiny of love to which he has called us.

Are you walking in integrity? Spend some time asking God about any areas of your life where you might feel compromised. What is God saying to you? And how will you respond?

SHEILA JACOBS

That woman!

Charm is deceptive, and beauty is fleeting; but a woman who fears the Lord is to be praised. Honour her for all that her hands have done, and let her works bring her praise at the city gate. (NIV)

Whether this list of womanly perfection found in the wife of noble character makes you cringe, or aspire to be such a person, it makes for fascinating reading. Here however, we are concentrating on some interesting contrasts.

The book of Proverbs spends some considerable time warning young men about the dangers of the adulteress. This could also be true in our time of the dangers posed by any romantic relationship – for men or women – that is going to lead nowhere good. It's difficult to see past charm at times, and it certainly can be deceptive.

It seems the young in particular are being judged on how they look and how attractive they are by today's standards. But 'beauty is fleeting' – even with the best products in the world, our appearance will inevitably change over time.

Here, we see the true worth of a woman (or any person!). The one who is to be praised is someone who 'fears the Lord'. It's the person who is seeking after God, who is trusting him and wanting to please him, who is living their life with integrity – which we thought about yesterday – who is to be honoured. Our works follow our faith. We are not saved by what we do, but by grace (Ephesians 2:8–9) – that is, God's unmerited, unearned favour. However, how we live out our lives will show what we truly believe.

Jesus said that we would recognise people by their fruit (Matthew 7:16, 20). What we believe internally displays itself in what we produce externally – our actions. If we are followers of Christ, then, even if we get it wrong at times, we will display his fruit in our lives.

Is your self-worth more about your inner life or your outward appearance? Think about it!

SHEILA JACOBS

Future hope

Do not let your heart envy sinners, but always be zealous for the fear of the Lord. There is surely a future hope for you, and your hope will not be cut off. (NIV)

Let's finish our travels in the book of Proverbs by looking at a wonderful promise of God – a future hope! In our reading today, we can see that the writer is issuing a warning: don't let your heart envy those in the world who do not know God. We need to be 'zealous' for the Lord. So, how do we keep that zeal alive in our hearts?

In these notes, we have been thinking about perspectives and focus. If we look at the things of the world, we can be drawn in, tempted to put God on the back burner so to speak, and before we know it, our thoughts, desires and ambitions are pretty much the same as the world's.

We need wisdom in how we live our lives. Perhaps, as we consider the different sayings in Proverbs, we may think some of them are not relevant to our lives. How wrong we would be; this book has so much to teach us about our attitude to wealth, the poor, relationships and simply 'living well'. We can find much treasure in its depths if we are prepared to do a little digging.

Proverbs 24:14 tells us that 'wisdom is like honey' and if we 'find it, there is a future hope for [us], and [our] hope will not be cut off'. Like honey, wisdom will bring goodness to our innermost being.

'Get wisdom, get understanding; do not forget my words or turn away from them' (4:5). Jesus Christ is himself 'wisdom from God' (1 Corinthians 1:30). Let's spend time with him, reading his word and learning from him as we listen to his 'gentle whisper' (1 Kings 19:12). The future, after all, is in the one who has the 'words of eternal life' (John 6:68).

Lord, help me to draw closer to you and to learn from you today. Thank you that you want me to walk more closely with you because you love me. Amen
SHEILA JACOBS

The kindness of God

Sandra Wheatley writes:

Our theme for the next two weeks is the kindness of God, and it has been a delight to delve more deeply into this attribute of God. It is seen time and time again throughout the Old and New Testaments, often enacted through familiar, and perhaps some unfamiliar, biblical characters as well as Jesus himself.

We are all, hopefully, familiar with kindness – it is defined as 'the quality of being friendly, generous and considerate' (*Oxford English Dictionary*). Each day, we have the opportunity to be kind to others: a smile to a passing stranger, opening the door to a burdened-down shopper or a kind word to a stressed-out mum.

Kindness is contagious, like a chain reaction, a wave that keeps on rolling. All it needs is one person to start it. Kindness is also intentional. We need to do those voluntary acts of kindness not only when it's easy to be kind, but also when it's hard to be.

A heroine of mine, the civil activist and poet Maya Angelou, said: 'Be a rainbow in someone else's cloud.' She said her life had had many clouds, but many more rainbows. Kindness, like a rainbow, can cast a different light and bring hope to those it touches. When someone is kind to us, we feel understood and seen.

In the Old Testament another word – *hesed* (or *chesed*) – is used to speak of God's kindness. Because no single English word can adequately encompass *hesed*, the Bible translates it as love, lovingkindness, goodness, favour, mercy, unfailing love, faithful love, steadfast love and unfailing kindness. What a word! It is so wonderful that God's *hesed* is all of these words, all at once and so much more.

It is also a distinctively covenantal word: God's covenant love for his people, Israel – and for us. We see his loyal and steadfast love tested to the limit many times in Old Testament stories. I am all too aware that God's love is tested in my life too.

As we explore the breadth and depth of God's kindness in the coming days, I hope your heart will be warmed by the kind embrace of God's amazing *hesed* for you!

A prayer before we begin: *Father God, thank you for this wonderful opportunity to read of your kindness flowing through the lives and events in scripture. Enable us to be channels of your kindness too. Amen*

Kindness all around

**You are kind, Lord, so good and merciful. You protect ordinary people.'
(CEV)**

The world can appear to be a hostile, dangerous and unkind place. The stories in news bulletins can make us wonder where kindness has gone as wars rage, famine increases and despair takes hold. Yet, in all we have witnessed or even suffered during the Covid-19 pandemic, the invasion of Ukraine and the worsening economic crisis, glimmers of kindness have still shone through.

What is it about kindness that makes it so powerful? Is it its simplicity – something we can do, say or demonstrate to anyone who crosses our path as we go about daily life? Or is it that when we are kind to others, we reflect something of God's character?

The rest of our reading says, 'You protect ordinary people, and when I was helpless you saved me and treated me so kindly that I don't need to worry anymore.' How wonderful is that! God treats ordinary people – you and me – kindly. But this kindness costs. God saw our need not only for protection, but also for salvation, and set in motion the means by which his kindness would draw us back to himself.

The most common Greek word for kindness is *chrestotes*, a wonderful play on *Christos* (Christ). God's kindness is embodied in Jesus, who came to live among us. He showed us the way to life, bringing us back to God, safe and protected forevermore.

We'll be exploring the lives of many ordinary people in scripture over the coming days to see how God shows his kindness to them and often reveals his kindness to others through them.

Father God, please help me to be aware of your kindness all around me today, in ordinary things and through ordinary people. Amen

SANDRA WHEATLEY

In the beginning

The Lord God made garments of skin for Adam and his wife and clothed them. (NIV)

The opening chapters of Genesis tell of our creator God and how he spoke the world into being. We read how he fashioned Adam from the dust of the earth and breathed life into him (Genesis 2:7) and how he created Eve from Adam's rib (Genesis 2:21–22) so that Adam wouldn't be alone. These first two chapters give us a glimpse of what could have been. Chapter 3 then details how humankind messed it all up because of their disobedience.

Our verse today, this small and seemingly insignificant verse, is part of that narrative. In what seems to have been a first for Adam and Eve, they hid from God. Their realisation that they were naked seemed to matter more than their disobedience. When God asked, 'Where are you?' it wasn't that he had lost them, but rather that they had thought they could hide from him.

Sometimes I have heard those words too. In times of confusion and uncertainty over a path I've taken, one that perhaps I shouldn't have, God's words, 'Where are you?' have brought me back to him, no longer confused or lost, but safe with him once again.

The kindness of God is displayed in this verse. He saw their shame; he knew their need. Before anything else, God made Adam and Eve garments of skin. That meant the sacrifice of an animal so that they could be clothed. This is the first instance of such a thing happening in scripture – and indicative of the sacrifice Jesus would make to redeem us and to 'clothe' us too in robes of redemption. Before God banished Adam and Eve from the garden that he had created for them, his kindness is displayed simply and effectively. It is what he does, it is who he is.

Thank you, God! You continue to seek us out when we drift away; you call us back to you and clothe us through your kindness and love. Amen

SANDRA WHEATLEY

Undeserved kindness

Jacob looked up and there was Esau, coming with his four hundred men. (NIV)

The incredible story of Jacob and Esau starts in chapter 25 and reads like a present-day soap opera! Younger brother Jacob takes Esau's birth right (25:29–34) and then through deceit takes his blessing from their dying father, Isaac (27:1–42). As a result, Jacob is forced to flee from home with Esau's words ringing in his ears: 'I will kill my brother Jacob' (27:41).

Twenty years later, God advised Jacob to return home (31:3). Jacob was clearly nervous about seeing his brother again and when he heard that Esau was coming to meet him with 400 men, he tried to pacify Esau with gifts ahead of their meeting (32:17–21). He was clearly terrified of what might happen. That night, Jacob had an encounter with God and what happened next was totally unexpected.

I recall situations in my life similar to Jacob's – not quite as life-threatening – when taking that step towards resolution, apology and forgiveness has been gut-wrenching and terrifying. As Jacob did, I would spend time with God, seeking his help and wisdom, but even so my stomach still churned as I anticipated what I knew I deserved.

As Jacob approached Esau and bowed before him, Esau didn't tear Jacob limb from limb; he didn't castigate and seek revenge. He ran to meet him, embraced him, thew his arms around his neck and kissed him. They wept together.

Esau's kindness towards Jacob banished the fear and dread, bringing reconciliation and peace at last. Jacob said: 'For to see your face is like seeing the face of God' (v. 10). When we encounter kindness, especially undeserved kindness, we too can see the face of God in those who have granted us this wonderful and most precious of gifts.

'Because of the Lord's great love we are not consumed, for his compassions never fail. They are new every morning; great is your faithfulness' (Lamentations 3:22–23).

SANDRA WHEATLEY

The implications of kindness

'Now then, please swear to me by the Lord that you will show kindness to my family, because I have shown kindness to you.' (NIV)

I had never noticed the little footnote that refers to Rahab's 'profession'. The NIV (1984) says, 'or possibly an innkeeper'. Amazingly throughout history Rahab is known more as a prostitute than an innkeeper!

It seems to have given this whole story a deeper meaning that a prostitute could shelter the spies sent by Joshua to suss out the city of Jericho before it was to be taken by the Israelites. But there she is, Rahab – a kind prostitute/innkeeper!

Rahab's kindness meant that the spies were safely hidden and could return to Joshua with the information needed so that when the time was right Jericho could be captured, and Rahab and her family would be safe (6:22–23).

Rahab became a godly wife and mother in Israel. She married Salmon, an Israelite from the tribe of Judah, and they had a baby boy named Boaz. Yes, the Boaz who was to be Ruth's kinsman redeemer!

The implications of Rahab's kindness are so significant – especially for those of us who often struggle to find our sense of place or self-worth. She is mentioned ten times in the Bible, one of which is Matthew 1:5 in the genealogy of Jesus. Jesus' family history includes all types of people. It includes dysfunctional families, addictions, anger and abuse. In short, it includes ordinary people just like you and me. The family Jesus came from tells us everything about the people Jesus came for! Someone once said: 'If we can identify and find ourselves with those named on that list, then we can find ourselves in the family of God.'

Rahab was kind and her actions meant that she became part of God's family. Kindness works!

Father God, thank you for inviting each one of us into your family. No matter what our past has been, you have given us a future in you. Amen

SANDRA WHEATLEY

The ripple effect of kindness

Then Naomi said to her two daughters-in-law, 'Go back, each of you, to your mother's home. May the Lord show you kindness, as you have shown kindness to your dead husbands and to me.' (NIV)

If ever there was a story that encapsulates God's kindness in scripture, it's the book of Ruth. It is only four chapters long. There is no account of battles being fought or awe-inspiring miracles happening. Instead, it reads like a quaint love story and is one of the few Bible stories told from a woman's viewpoint. It almost seems out of place, and yet God's lovingkindness shines in each detail of the narrative.

The backdrop to the story is famine, cross-cultural marriage and tragedy. Ruth shows deep loyalty to her widowed mother-in-law, Naomi (1:16–17) and the two widowed women, in different seasons of life, come together to journey back from Moab to Naomi's home and kinsmen in Bethlehem.

If you have time, do read the book of Ruth. It really is a wonderful story of love and friendship – and it encapsulates our theme. We see what can happen when one person is kind to another. Ruth's kindness towards Naomi (2:18) ripples through the story, but we also see Naomi's kindness to Ruth (1:11–12, 3:1), Boaz's kindness towards Ruth (2:15–16) and hers to him (3:7–11). Small tokens of kindness are spoken of throughout the story, each one drawing Ruth and Boaz ever closer into a relationship and marriage which would also place them into the incredible genealogy of Jesus (Matthew 1:5). It is those seemingly random acts of kindness that result in Ruth and Boaz playing such a significant part in Jesus' family history.

I'm challenged to actively seek out opportunities in which I can share not only random acts of kindness, but extravagant acts of kindness each day!

Father God, in my relationships and friendships, help me to pass on the kindnesses I have received so that a ripple of kindness flows through my day. Amen

SANDRA WHEATLEY

The power of kindness

Then David accepted from her hand what she had brought to him and said, 'Go home in peace. I have heard your words and granted your request.' (NIV)

In our readings so far, we've seen kindness triumph over the harsh reality of the breakdown of relationships, being shared by those with a sullied reputation and lavished upon a refugee and a widow.

Now we read about David, a 'man after [God's] own heart' (13:14) – a shepherd, fugitive, king and psalmist. He was the great-grandson of Ruth and Boaz and of the many instances of kindness he experienced, I will focus on Abigail's kindness towards him when he was a fugitive, on the run from King Saul.

This chapter is unusual because a woman is the main character, and her speech (vv. 24–31) is one of the longest by any woman in scripture. Abigail was astute, as well as intelligent, beautiful and brave (v. 3). When the servants told her of her husband's refusal to help David, her quick-thinking and immensely kind actions really did save the day. We see here the power of kindness. Abigail asked that David remember her, and he did (vv. 39–42), especially her act of kindness.

In many of the psalms David wrote, he speaks of the kindness or loving-kindness of God. This is particularly noticeable in those written when he was on the run from the jealous, ruthless King Saul.

I wonder if he recalled this meeting with Abigail when he wrote: 'You provide delicious food for me in the presence of my enemies... Your goodness and unfailing kindness shall be with me all of my life' (Psalm 23:5–6, TLB). Did the kindness Abigail showed David remind him of the unfailing kindness of God? Can the kindness we show others today remind them of the kindness of God too? I hope so.

The bravery and kindness of Abigail averted certain bloodshed! Have there been times in your life when an opportunity to intervene in a crisis with a kind word or action has saved the day?

SANDRA WHEATLEY

A kind invitation

'Is there anyone still left of the house of Saul to whom I can show kindness for Jonathan's sake?' (NIV)

I love this story. David's days of hiding from Saul are over. Saul and his son, David's dear friend Jonathan, are dead. David is king, and he recalls a covenant made between him and Jonathan (1 Samuel 20:13–17). David asks the question in verse 1 of today's passage, not only to fulfil a promise, but also to show kindness.

He is told that Jonathan has a disabled son, Mephibosheth (4:4), who is brought to David and welcomed as if he were his own son. Mephibosheth is given a seat at David's table and provision for life. What an honour! What kindness!

This incredible story is an analogy of God's kindness to us all. When Mephibosheth suffered a fall, he was disabled for the rest of his life. When sin entered the world, humanity suffered a 'fall' which left us spiritually less able to follow God's perfect law. Just as David sought out Mephibosheth to show him kindness, God extends his unconditional acceptance to us through Jesus' death on the cross, and God continues to seek us out.

I am touched by this story because I have known discrimination and verbal abuse as a disabled person. I'm often overlooked and made to feel I have no worth or value. When I was first diagnosed with MS, the church I attended forgot about me and I faded from view. I felt alone and bereft. However, as new friends came into my life, I began to see God's kindness again, especially when I was invited into their homes to share a meal with them. It is a simple gesture, but like David's kindness to Mephibosheth, it means so much.

Father God, thank you! Your invitation through Jesus' death and resurrection to come to your table and dine with you still stands – for anyone and everyone. Amen

SANDRA WHEATLEY

Kindness to the weary

The angel of the Lord came back a second time and touched him and said, 'Get up and eat, for the journey is too much for you.' (NIV)

Today we meet Elijah, a prophet of God who was exhausted, despondent and ready to call it a day. He was sitting under a broom tree, praying that he might die: 'I have had enough, Lord,' he says, 'Take my life' (v. 4). Too weary to continue, he fell asleep.

This is a story that resonates, doesn't it? It may be pressures of life, a demanding ministry or job, family conflicts or the challenge of caring for a loved one, but what was once a daily privilege becomes an exhausting daily grind. 'I've had enough, Lord' is a plea from the heart.

Elijah was woken by an angel of the Lord. Through bleary eyes he saw a jar of water and bread baked on hot coals. He ate and drank and slept again. After another nap, the angel of the Lord returned, encouraged Elijah to eat a little more and then guided him to an incredible encounter with God on Mount Horeb (19:11–13).

What kindness God showed to a weary and exhausted soul! He did the same for Hagar (Genesis 21:14–19), when she was too exhausted to continue her journey in the desert.

I have no way of knowing how you may be feeling today, but God does. If you, like Elijah, have had enough and can't even imagine taking another step, please stop and rest, even for a moment. My prayer as I write these words is that you too will experience the kindness of God today. Let him bring you all that you need practically, physically or spiritually. Listen for his gentle whisper and let him envelop you in his kindness.

Father, please draw those who are feeling weary and worn out to your green pastures and still waters. Refresh them and strengthen them for the journey ahead. Amen

SANDRA WHEATLEY

The epitome of kindness

But when the kindness and love of God our Saviour appeared, he saved us, not because of righteous things we had done, but because of his mercy. (NIV)

What a wonderful verse! Here is kindness, embodied in Jesus, God's Son, our Saviour.

The Greek word for kindness is *chrestotes*. Tertullian, an early Christian author and church father, wrote that pagans called the early Christians by the name *Chrestiani*, which means *kindness*. It is closely associated with the word *Christiani*, Christian, yet it was kindness that set the early Christians apart.

How I long for that to be said of me. I try to look out for opportunities to show kindness to those I encounter each day: opening a door for someone, sharing food, sending a card, calling someone on the phone or chatting to the person on the checkout. The opportunities seem endless, but is the fruit of kindness (Galatians 5:22) flourishing in my life?

We show kindness when we treat other people deferentially, going beyond being merely polite or nice, in order to gently and tenderly extend warmth and love. Kindness involves a generosity of spirit, a desire to say or do something that ennobles another person and makes them feel cared for and cherished.

It is quite a challenge, isn't it? Yet there was new emergence of kindness amid all we faced during the Covid-19 lockdowns. The BBC even commissioned a study on kindness in 2022 which 60,000 people responded to! It seems that kindness is in vogue.

Our passage today reminds us that the kindness of God is at the very core of our salvation. As Christians, it is Jesus' love that motivates us to show kindness to others, however and whenever we can. Even if we feel that the 'milk of human kindness' sometimes seems a little curdled, we are called to follow Jesus' example and make a difference.

Father God, when I choose to be kind to others, I feel good inside; when I miss an opportunity, I feel sad. Help me to make the right choice today to pass on the kindness I've received from you. Amen

SANDRA WHEATLEY

Touched by kindness

Jesus reached out his hand and touched the man, 'I am willing,' he said. (NIV)

When Jesus lived on earth, leprosy was the worst of all plagues. It was seen as a filthy, deadly disease from which no one recovered. More frightening still was that it spread arbitrarily and wildly, with no cure and no hope. The moment a leprous lesion appeared on them, a beloved family member became a social outcast – isolated, rejected, feared and despised. Whole chapters of the law focused on instructing the Israelites how to deal with a leper (Leviticus 13—14).

Jesus' encounter with this man with leprosy was remarkable. I imagine as he approached Jesus there may have been a mini stampede as the other people present tried to move as far away as possible. It was a courageous move by a desperate man.

The man's plea to Jesus was met with another remarkable response. Not only did Jesus respond verbally, 'I am willing. Be clean', but he also reached out and touched the man! This despised, untouchable man was touched by kindness and grace. He may not have known such kindness for years. In touching him, Jesus broke all laws and boundaries set by society. Jesus shows that simple, kind touch can bring healing and wholeness. How can we do the same?

When I worked as a nurse, appropriate touch was integral to all that we did. It was seen as vital to touch our patients, to hold a hand and to give support and care through a gentle touch.

I know from personal experience that when we don't know what to say, a simple touch can restore hope and alleviate loneliness and isolation. Let's not underestimate the power of touch and the difference it can make.

Father God, restore to us the confidence to reach out and touch others when appropriate. May we always be ready to bring your comfort and care to those around us. Amen

SANDRA WHEATLEY

Sought out by kindness

There is neither Jew nor Gentile, neither slave nor free, nor is there male and female, for you are all one in Christ Jesus. (NIV)

There is a prayer still prayed by Orthodox Rabbis: 'Blessed are you, our God, ruler of the universe, for not making me a Gentile, slave, or woman.' Jesus knew that prayer, yet he sought women out.

There are three familiar stories that show how Jesus' lovingkindness radically transformed the lives of women who were outcasts, vilified and shunned: the woman at the well (John 4:4–42), the bleeding woman (Luke 8:41–48) and the woman caught in adultery (John 8:1–11).

There may be aspects of their stories that resonate with us. Perhaps we feel isolated because of our circumstances and long for someone to tell us it's okay and to assure us that we are known and loved. Maybe we have a dark secret that keeps us from enjoying close relationships and friendships, fearing we're not good enough or that if people knew who we really were, they wouldn't like us. Yet that longing to touch and be touched, to know kindness and healing through acceptance gnaws at us daily.

Or perhaps we feel exposed and vulnerable. Our actions have resulted in humiliation and judgement. How can we ever feel whole, forgiven or loved when what we have done has revealed so much about us?

In each of these encounters, Jesus treated the women with dignity and kindness. He didn't judge a thirsty woman, he didn't push away one longing to know a healing touch and he didn't join a gawping, baying crowd bent on bloodshed and judgement.

Jesus broke with every convention of his day when he engaged with these women and brought hope for a better future to each of them. He still does. He still will.

Reflect on these words from 'Here is love' by William Rees (1802–83): 'Grace and love, like mighty rivers, poured incessant from above, and heaven's peace and perfect justice kissed a guilty world in love.'

SANDRA WHEATLEY

Extravagant kindness

Then turning to the woman, but speaking to Simon, he said, 'Do you see this woman? I came to your home; you provided no water for my feet, but she rained tears on my feet and dried them with her hair… she has soothed my feet with perfume.' (MSG)

The other three gospels also all have an account of the washing of Jesus' feet by a woman: Matthew 26:6–13, Mark 14:3–9, John 12:1–8. The accounts are very similar, but it is the detail in Luke's story that demonstrates not only this woman's immense sense of gratitude, but also the opportunity she took to be kind to Jesus.

Kindness is often quiet and behind the scenes; it can go unnoticed except to the giver and the recipient. Not so in this instance!

Jesus had accepted Simon the Pharisee's invitation to dinner. This may well have been quite a gathering and included many of Simon's fellow Pharisees, who were seeking an opportunity to question Jesus or catch him out. One person not on the invitation list was this woman, referred to as the 'town harlot' (v. 37) – clearly a woman of ill-repute!

As Jesus reclined at the table, she stood behind him and wept – so much so that her tears started to drench Jesus' feet. She then used her hair to dry his feet, kissing them and pouring perfume on them. The room filled with the aroma of the expensive perfume – and the disdain of the other guests.

Jesus pointed out to Simon what her actions meant (vv. 44–46). Simon had failed to offer even the most basic courtesy to Jesus, but this woman had shown great kindness and care.

In the other gospel accounts, those present questioned the use of expensive, precious perfume in this way. How wrong they were; no act of kindness is ever a waste. The way we treat others is our way of showing kindness to Jesus (Matthew 25:35–40).

Father God, when I encounter the hungry, the thirsty, the stranger, the sick or the imprisoned today, may I recognise you and take the opportunity to be kind. Amen

SANDRA WHEATLEY

Radical kindness

Jesus said, 'Father, forgive them, for they do not know what they are doing.' (NIV)

The death, burial and resurrection of Jesus Christ is the ultimate demonstration of the kindness of God. He gave his Son that we might live. The radical kindness shown by Jesus here makes the kindness we may encounter – a cup of tea being made for us, a kind word, a gesture that assures us we're doing okay – seem small in comparison.

To die as Jesus did and in the very process to speak such words of kindness is beyond our comprehension. We see Jesus responding to the thief being crucified alongside him, giving him hope of a new life (vv. 39–43). Then, seeing his mother and John watching and weeping, Jesus brings them together: '"Woman, here is your son", and to the disciple [John], "Here is your mother"' (John 19:26–27). Jesus is ensuring his mum would be cared for and not alone. Jesus died as he had lived, showing lovingkindness to others.

Out of the brutality and horror of the crucifixion, Jesus literally pours out kindness as his life blood was shed. And we, too, are the recipients of his kindness, for Jesus died that we might be forgiven, freed from the power of sin and reconciled to God. Take a moment to reflect on everything God has done for us and if this is the first time you have encountered the kindness of God's forgiveness through Jesus' death on the cross, please don't let this moment pass. This is your moment to receive forgiveness, wholeness and new life. Jesus loves you and wants you to know him.

'Jesus… soften my step, and still my mind; so may your presence of peace be over me. Peace be here; my heart is open' (The Northumbria Community, Celtic Daily Prayer Book Two: Farther up and farther in, William Collins, 2015).
SANDRA WHEATLEY

Being kind

Be kind and compassionate to one another, forgiving one another, just as in Christ God forgave you. (NIV)

There are over 200 instances of kindness in the Bible! I feel that I have barely scratched the surface in writing these notes on the kindness of God. There are so many places in scripture that encourage us, challenge us and affirm for us that being kind is not only a fruit of the Spirit (Galatians 5:22–23) but also a wave that keeps on rolling.

I hope you have been encouraged to see that what God started in the garden of Eden and what Jesus fulfilled on the cross continues to flow into and out of our lives; that the simplest, smallest acts of kindness can transform a situation and change lives.

I am reminded of the early days of the war in Ukraine when glimmers of kindness amid the horrors of war reduced me to tears: news footage of Ukrainian mothers offering surrendered young Russian soldiers a cup of tea and the use of their mobile phones to call their mums in Russia; Poland and Latvia opening their borders to receive the millions of fleeing women and children; and the prayers and the aid that flooded across Europe. It may well be that wars continue, famines worsen and the world may seem out of control, but one thing will remain – the kindness and love of God. It is our turn now to pass on what we have received from him. Monday 13 November is World Kindness Day. Let's be radical and try to fill every day with kindness.

'There are three things that are important in human life. The first is to be kind, the second is to be kind, the third is to be kind.' – Anon.

Father God, your lovingkindness envelops us every day. May we have the courage to pass on all that we have received in simple and random acts of kindness. Amen

SANDRA WHEATLEY

Praying with David

Amy Boucher Pye writes:

David was far from perfect – he was an adulterer and a murderer – but God fully forgave him. A man of prayer, he gave us many of the words and poetry that have resonated with millions over the centuries in the Psalms, the prayer book of the Bible. I can't imagine life without his prayers!

Over the next two weeks, we will join David as he expresses praise and worship, glory and honour to God. We'll also see him cry out to God in pain and anguish as he seeks help and deliverance from the loving and saving Lord. David holds nothing back from God, which should encourage us to share all of our hopes and dreams, and our disappointment and sadness, with the one who made us.

Throughout this fortnight we'll see hints of David's circumstances, whether he's on the run from his son Absalom or rejoicing that King Saul didn't succeed with his death threats; but we'll also notice how often he majors on God and leaves the specifics out of his cries to the Lord. For example, in Psalm 51, the famous song of confession and repentance after he takes Bathsheba for his own pleasure and then arranges the murder of her husband, he doesn't mention any of that wrongdoing to God. He understands that God already knows all of the specifics; he wants his loving Father to erase the sin that he committed specifically against him.

We start with one of David's prayers outside of the Psalms, when he's dedicating the materials for what will be the new house of God. We then move to the Psalms as we join David in praising God, praying for deliverance and peace, crying to him in trouble, waiting for him, confessing our sins, depending on him, longing for God and finding rest in him.

I pray that you will find this foray into David's words helpful and encouraging as you express to God what's on your heart and your mind. Know that you can share with God anything and everything that you're feeling and experiencing. May you encounter the living, loving Lord, the one who finds joy and pleasure when you turn to him.

Dedicating ourselves to God

'Praise be to you, Lord, the God of our father Israel, from everlasting to everlasting. Yours, Lord, is the greatness and the power and the glory and the majesty and the splendour, for everything in heaven and earth is yours.' (NIV)

We begin at the end. David's life was marked by prayer, and one of his last acts was to gather all the materials for his son Solomon to build the temple, the place where God's presence would dwell. After receiving the amazing outpouring of gifts, including gold and silver for the lampstands, tables and basins, he prays a prayer of dedication that still resounds with us today.

Note how David's prayer breaks into four sections as he first offers praises to God in naming who he is and his amazing attributes (vv. 10–12), then he moves on to giving thanks before this mighty God (vv. 13–16) and then puts his requests before God, seeking his continued influence and grace in the lives of his people as he hands over his life's work to his son (vv. 17–19). He concludes his prayer with a call to those assembled to worship and praise in humility (v. 20). This prayer has reverberated throughout the centuries, and parts of it continue in many liturgies of praise even today.

Why not spend some time praying back David's words of dedication? You could write out the prayer in your own words as a way of making it your own. As you do so, note how David focuses on God as the source of all good things – David doesn't claim any of the glory or the honour for the gathering of the riches. You could follow David's example of naming the things you want to give back to God, whether material items or something more intangible, such as your energy and devotion. You could ask God to help you list the ways he's given to you abundantly, which, if you're feeling a lack in some area, might help you to sense God's love and care.

Know that our great and exalted God is your Father, and that he will help you keep your heart loyal to him.

Praise to you, Lord! You are majestic and wonderful, and I exalt your name. Help me to bow down before you and honour you with my whole heart. Amen
AMY BOUCHER PYE

Praising God

'Hear, Lord, and be merciful to me; Lord, be my help.' You turned my wailing into dancing; you removed my sackcloth and clothed me with joy, that my heart may sing your praises and not be silent. Lord my God, I will praise you forever. (NIV)

Have you noticed when you're in the pit of despair – over a failed relationship, an unfulfilled dream or a seemingly insurmountable problem – how God can turn your wailing into dancing, even if it takes a very long time? When I sink into sadness, I try to remember how God previously brought me joy and peace. I may not experience any hopeful emotions just then, but I know that God can restore them to me – eventually. This is what the psalmist expresses in this song, how the wailing can last into the night but how rejoicing comes in the morning.

Unlike in our modern Bibles, in the original setting the psalm's opening heading would not be separated from the text of the song and would be seen as a critical part of the whole. It indicates that David wrote it for the dedication of the temple. David had died by the time the temple had been built, so some biblical commentators believe that he wrote it while anticipating its completion. Notice though how he never mentions the temple. Rather, his is a song of praise and thanksgiving that he offers even while he suffers.

We can use the heading's word 'dedication' to help us rededicate ourselves to God. As we experience the depths of pain (v. 1), we can trust that God will lift us up and that he will heal us (v. 2). He will help us to sing his praises (v. 4) and to stand firm on his promises (v. 7). We cry to the Lord for mercy (v. 8), asking him to be our help (v. 10). He will answer, clothing us in joy (v. 11).

May you know renewed hope and peace as you trust in God.

Loving God, I know you care for me, even when things happen that shake my trust in you. Restore to me the hope and joy of my salvation. Amen
AMY BOUCHER PYE

Praying for deliverance and peace

But you, Lord, are a shield around me, my glory, the One who lifts my head high. I call out to the Lord, and he answers me from his holy mountain. I lie down and sleep; I wake again, because the Lord sustains me. (NIV)

Actions have consequences, and the sins that we commit can transfer to those close to us. For instance, I can trace some of the stubbornness I see in my kids back to me and how unyielding I am at times. King David certainly had issues with his children, which blew up when his son Absalom rebelled. You can read the full story in 2 Samuel, but in short, his coercion of Bathsheba into sexual sin was followed by the rape of his daughter Tamar by Amon, her half-brother, which was then followed by retribution from her brother Absalom. Yes, it's complicated, and very messy.

Although David had wreaked havoc in his family affairs with very poor choices, he did return to God again and again. In this psalm, he's running from his incensed son because he fears for his life. I can imagine David fretting through the night over the whole mess, but he cries out to God for help (v. 4). The next morning he reports that God gave him a good night's sleep (v. 5). Such is the faithfulness of God.

David keeps on turning to God for deliverance and help (v. 7). Although his foes are many (v. 1), God is a shield around him (v. 3). This imagery would have held a deep meaning for David as he would anticipate holding up a physical shield against the arrows of his beloved enemy.

Whatever the ramifications of our own sin in the lives of those close to us, we can join David in returning to God. As we look to him for help and deliverance, he will respond; with the first answer to prayer perhaps being a glorious full night of sleep.

Loving God, I fail you so often, but you graciously restore me again and again. Please put right the messes that my unfaithfulness creates and make my heart pure. Amen

AMY BOUCHER PYE

Crying out to God in trouble

I cry aloud to the Lord; I lift up my voice to the Lord for mercy. I pour out before him my complaint; before him I tell my trouble. When my spirit grows faint within me, it is you who watch over my way. (NIV)

Entering the small opening in the rocks, the cool air envelops me as my eyes take a moment to adjust. I'm breathing fast, my anxiety quickening my heartrate, while also feeling emotionally spent. *Where is God? Why I am so alone?* I sink to the ground, thinking that no one cares for my life. I pour out my complaints to God.

That's an imagining of what David experienced in the cave when he wrote this psalm, and I hope it helps you picture yourself in similar circumstances. David had two cave experiences when he was on the run and had to hide away (see 1 Samuel 22:1 and 24:3). In this instance, he is alone and turns to God in prayer, crying out to him with his burdens, requests and praises.

Spend a few moments pondering the opening verses of this psalm. In Hebrew, the 'cry' in the first verse has the sense of shrieking with terror – David clearly fears for his life, enough to leave the comforts of the palace to hide out in an isolated cave. Then he follows his vocal outburst with requesting God's mercy. He knows that only God can deliver him. He feels completely comfortable telling every little thing to God – he names his complaints and recounts his troubles (v. 2).

If we feel shy about sharing all our concerns with God, we can take heart from this song by one known as a man after God's own heart (see 1 Samuel 13:14). Just as he named the things that he struggled with, we too can present God with all our fears, anxieties, sadness and pain. Of course, we can also offer him our praises, words of worship and honour and rejoicing.

Loving God, you welcome me to give you both my burdens and my praises. Help me to train myself to converse with you throughout the moments of my day. Amen

AMY BOUCHER PYE

Praising God when under pressure

Have mercy on me, my God, have mercy on me, for in you I take refuge. I will take refuge in the shadow of your wings until the disaster has passed. I cry out to God Most High, to God, who vindicates me. (NIV)

Have you ever experienced the seemingly miraculous change that God sparks as an answer to prayer? One moment you're wracked with pain and fear and then, after you've prayed – perhaps with a trusted friend – you feel a wave of peace. Your circumstances haven't shifted but something within you has. When God moves within me like this, I'm so grateful.

We can chart David's expression of trust throughout this psalm. Again, David is in a cave – perhaps we can glean from this setting that arduous and angst-ridden circumstances can bring about a depth and richness to our prayers. He asks for God's mercy and shares how he will take refuge in God, even though trouble presses on him on every side. He knows that God alone will save him.

Note how the psalm splits into two with the same refrain in verse 5 and 11 as David expresses reverence for the great God above the heavens. The repeated words remind us that this is a song, but they also point David to trust in the creator, the one who made him and who can save him from the marauding lions.

What ravenous beasts are coming towards you? We may not feel that we're in direct conflict such as David experienced, but we may have to contend with physical maladies, mental health issues, relationship troubles, financial struggles or feelings of hopelessness. All these conflicts and challenges can sap us of our strength and our faith; but we can join David in putting our confidence in God and affirming that our hearts are steadfast within us. Know that God's love reaches to the heavens, his faithfulness to the skies.

Gracious God, when I am feeling low and attacked, please help me to put my confidence in you. You are exalted above all else; your glory fills the skies. Amen

AMY BOUCHER PYE

Waiting for God

Hear my voice when I call, Lord; be merciful to me and answer me. My heart says of you, 'Seek his face!' Your face, Lord, I will seek. Do not hide your face from me, do not turn your servant away in anger; you have been my helper. (NIV)

At the beginning of the year, I like to choose a word and a passage from scripture to focus on. Some years ago, my verse was Psalm 27:14: 'Wait for the Lord; be strong and take heart and wait for the Lord.' I would turn it round and round in my head as I waited for God to deliver on the desires of my heart. When nothing seemed to happen, I found comfort in the verbs in this verse. Waiting wasn't an empty and passive practice, but one in which I could be strong and stay encouraged as I held on. The phrase 'take heart' conveys a striking image – we can picture ourselves taking hold of our hearts as we instruct our emotions on how to wait for our good and gracious God.

David starts off his song by expressing his confidence in God. He's got reason to fear because of his foes, but from his experience he knows that God will come through for him. He will be confident (v. 3). Spending time in God's house – not only in heaven but here on earth – will help him through his troubles (vv. 4–6). He then moves on to direct requests of God – don't hide your face from me and don't reject me (v. 9); teach me your ways (v. 11); and don't let my enemies win (v. 12).

What are you waiting for? What desires and hopes could you lay before God today while you express your confidence in him? You might have some buried dreams that you fear God might ignore or decline. Ask God to show them to you as you seek his wisdom and guidance about whether they are ones to cling to or ones to relinquish. May God keep us strong in heart as we wait.

Teach me to wait, Lord, and help me not to lose confidence in you. Strengthen my faith – build my foundation so deep that I won't waver when I face challenges and difficulties. Amen

AMY BOUCHER PYE

Confessing and repenting

Have mercy on me, O God, according to your unfailing love; according to your great compassion blot out my transgressions. Wash away all my iniquity and cleanse me from my sin. For I know my transgressions, and my sin is always before me. (NIV)

King David makes a key mistake when he decides not to join his troops in war and instead stays home at the palace. Lusting over the woman on the next rooftop, he demands her presence and uses her for his pleasure. When she becomes pregnant, he adds the descriptor of murderer to adulterer. This lauded man of God takes a mighty fall with consequences that ripple through many generations.

This psalm expresses his deep repentance for his actions. Notice how although the heading describes the events of 2 Samuel 11, David doesn't recount them here. Rather he names his sins and iniquities against God. He's doing the deep heart-work of confession and repentance as he acknowledges that only God can forgive him fully, as much as he should also seek forgiveness from Bathsheba and others.

The verb 'cleanse' in verse 7 has an interesting connotation in the Hebrew (*katharizo*) in that it means 'de-sin'. David asks God to remove so completely his horrible actions that every last trace of them disappears. We can decontaminate things in the English language, but we don't typically speak of de-sinning – perhaps we should! There's a visual sense to this term that I rather like.

Why not read through this passage a few times, asking God to reveal to you any hidden sins or wrongdoing? You could chew over a word or phrase that pops out to you, speaking it back to God as you apply it to your situation. While doing so, make sure that you take enough time to hear from God and rest in his presence too. He longs to meet with us and set us free from our sins.

Against you do I do wrong, Lord. De-sin me that I might stand before you without any blemish or stain. Create in me a pure heart, O God, and renew a right spirit within me. Amen

AMY BOUCHER PYE

Seeking forgiveness and guidance

All the ways of the Lord are loving and faithful toward those who keep the demands of his covenant. For the sake of your name, Lord, forgive my iniquity, though it is great. Who, then, are those who fear the Lord? (NIV)

I delight in finding different ways to pray. One such practice is praying through the alphabet. That is, I start off a line of prayer with the first letter of the alphabet, followed by the next and so on. Our psalm today is the first instance of such a way of praying in the Psalms, known as an acrostic poem.

Most of us won't know the original language here, so the way our translation moves through the verses might feel more disjointed to us than it would to the original reader. Nevertheless, we can benefit from trying out this practice in our own lives – even if you don't have time today, might you include praying through the alphabet sometime this week?

Verse 11 is the pivot point in this psalm, and in it David asks God to relieve him of his sins – his iniquity, which is the more old-fashioned but evocative term. This word in Hebrew has the sense of intentional action, that which is crooked and wrong. In asking God for guidance, David knows that his sinning will block the way for him to live a life that is pleasing to God. So he wants God to remove it from him.

What decisions press in on your heart and mind just now? Spend some moments asking God if you have some unconfessed wrongdoing lurking in the background that might keep you from seeking his help and guidance for the way forward. Know that he will delight to release you of any hurtful actions or thoughts that might be clouding your relationship with him and others.

Loving God, I know that sometimes I ignore those things I've done wrong, wanting to brush them under the carpet. Reveal them to me, that I might confess them and find forgiveness and freedom. Amen

AMY BOUCHER PYE

Praying when distressed

How long will you love delusions and seek false gods? Know that the Lord has set apart his faithful servant for himself; the Lord hears when I call to him. Tremble and do not sin; when you are on your beds, search your hearts and be silent. (NIV)

As I write, the UK experiences its hottest day ever. An airport runway melted and railway tracks buckled. When I walk by the nearby brook, I'm saddened to see it depleted of water. I think of the effect of this heat on the crops, not only here but also in Europe, where wildfires rage. In these circumstances and others such as rising prices of food and fuel, will we trust in God?

David writes this psalm in the midst of severe droughts. Rains haven't come and the crops are failing, and God's people are tempted to trust in false gods – those who promise the fertility of land and people. David cries out to God over the faithlessness of the people (v. 1) before admonishing them to return to the true God (v. 2 onwards). In this context, he says, 'Tremble and do not sin' (v. 4). The word 'tremble' invokes a sense of shaking as during an earthquake or in the presence of the holy God. Thus, David instructs the people to stay true to God, even though emotions erupt within them.

David acknowledges that we will experience a range of emotions, but he longs that we won't become slaves to them. We can exercise restraint and keep our hearts pure as we worship and serve God. Of course, this is easier said than done, whether not having to have the last word in a discussion or not responding in anger when provoked.

As we pray along with David, we will find help to overcome our errant ways – shine your face on me (v. 6); 'fill my heart with joy' (v. 7); I'll lie down in peace and sleep as I dwell in safety (v. 8). May it be so for you and for me.

Lord, help me to rein in my emotions, that I wouldn't be a slave to them. I want to stand pure before you, and I need your help to do so. Amen

AMY BOUCHER PYE

Turning to God

But you, Lord, are a compassionate and gracious God, slow to anger, abounding in love and faithfulness. Turn to me and have mercy on me; show your strength on behalf of your servant; save me, because I serve you just as my mother did. (NIV)

So often when we're crushed by our circumstances – the people whispering about us, the lack of opportunities, the betrayal of loved ones, our health concerns – we issue long complaints to God about what's going on. He welcomes any and all of our prayers, but in those tough times we can also list God's attributes. In doing so we turn our gaze from ourselves to God; and often we will find peace, objectivity and hope.

This is how David writes this song. He's being assailed by enemies, but he leaves his circumstances to the end. Instead of majoring on the troubles before him, he reminds God of God's qualities while he asks for mercy. Note, for instance, how he says in verse 5 that the Lord is forgiving and good, and that he abounds in love to all who call on him; that God hears the cries of the distressed (v. 7) and among the gods there is none like the true and living God (v. 8).

After proclaiming God's good nature, David turns to praying about himself. He wants God to teach him his ways and to give him a clear purpose (v. 11) while giving all the glory to God (v. 12). After noting the troubles he's in (v. 14), he again reminds God of who he is – compassionate, gracious, slow to anger, abounding in love and faithfulness (v. 15). How could a God like this abandon him? By his very nature, he won't. So David asks him to save him (v. 16) as he seeks a sign of God's goodness that will be seen by his enemies and put them to shame (v. 17).

Why not write out those attributes of God we see in our passage today, that you might cling to them and let them settle from your head to your heart?

You, Lord, are gracious and compassionate. You're slow to anger and rich in love. You who reign over all the world, reign in my heart. Amen

AMY BOUCHER PYE

Longing for God

You, God, are my God, earnestly I seek you; I thirst for you, my whole being longs for you, in a dry and parched land where there is no water. I have seen you in the sanctuary and beheld your power and your glory. (NIV)

In my 20s, when recovering from an unhealthy relationship, I wanted to seek God's love over that of a man's. To focus on God, I made this psalm my own. As I read it, even memorising it, I'd pour out my longings for love to God, earnestly seeking him. David's imagery of thirsting for God resonated with me as I'd wake early and pour over the scriptures, awed that this loving God knew me so intimately and loved me.

David wrote these words when he was on the move, probably when he was fleeing King Saul. Finding himself in a dry and weary land, he turns to God to quench his thirst. He seeks God as a person in the desert makes a concerted search for water. When David recounts how he's seen God in the sanctuary (v. 2), he uses a verb in the original language that is less common than the usual one. The one he employs has the sense of experiencing a vision of God. This interaction with God in the temple stays with him and encourages him when he is in the desert alone, isolated and in trouble.

Whereas in other psalms, such as Psalm 3 when David expresses his thanks for a good night of sleep, here he's awake during the night (v. 6). He's not complaining about the lack of sleep but uses the time to commune with God. Through his time of prayer, even in the night, he finds a deep satisfaction. His prayers nourish him like good food (v. 5).

I echo David's declaration: God, you are my God; earnestly I seek you. Join me in voicing these prayers to our loving God.

Lord, I thirst for you and seek for you throughout the day and the night. You are my help; I sing to you in the shadow of your wings. Amen

AMY BOUCHER PYE

Expressing all our feelings to God

But as for me, afflicted and in pain – may your salvation, God, protect me. I will praise God's name in song and glorify him with thanksgiving. (NIV)

We might find part of this psalm uncomfortable – it's one of those known by the technical term of the imprecatory psalms, which call on God to exercise judgement or curses on those spreading evil. We might cringe to read statements such as, 'Pour out your wrath on them' (v. 24) or 'May their eyes be darkened so that they cannot see' (v. 23).

Such songs form an important part of the honest cries of David. Without holding anything back from God, and instead of seeking revenge himself, David states all the things he wants God to do. He leaves the vengeance to God.

Notice the shift from his cries of pain and torment to verse 30, where he declares that he will praise and give thanks to God. His pivot is so quick that we might get a bit of emotional whiplash as we read and pray along with him. He's released all his anguish to God and has put the matter into the hands of the One who can do something about it. He's then content to offer thanks and praise, knowing that 'the Lord hears the needy' (v. 33).

We too can give every thought and feeling to God, even the messy ones. It's Thanksgiving in the USA today and this can feel complicated for me as an American living in Britain. Being away from family on Thanksgiving can make me sad, but I can express all my mixed feelings to God as I then turn to thanks – for my wonderful, adopted country and its people, for the gracious hosting of St Paul's Cathedral of a service for Americans and so many other blessings.

What jumble of feelings might you offer to God today? Trust that he loves to hear all of them.

Lord, I'm reluctant to call fire down on my enemies! But I want to be honest with you and share all that I am feeling. Please help me to be honest, knowing that you receive all of my prayers. Amen

AMY BOUCHER PYE

Finding rest in God

Yes, my soul, find rest in God; my hope comes from him. Truly he is my rock and my salvation; he is my fortress, I shall not be shaken. My salvation and my honour depend on God; he is my mighty rock, my refuge. (NIV)

After a broken night of sleep, we wake, groggy and disorientated. We might feel agitated and snappy, our nerves on edge. Or we might slowly emerge from the fog of sleep, feeling as if we're wading in treacle. We've not found rest for our bodies or for our souls.

In this psalm, David looks to God for true restorative rest. Note how he starts off in verse 1 by declaring how his soul finds rest in God, and then how in verse 5 he shifts the emphasis while repeating that statement, this time addressing himself ('Yes, my soul, find rest in God'). He's instructing his soul how to act in these circumstances.

We often need to follow David's example in this education of our souls. Many times – such as after a particularly sleepless night – we can easily descend into irritability and hopelessness. But as we remind ourselves of the truths of God, that he's our rock and salvation, we can tell ourselves to place our hope in God. We don't have to fall foul of our wayward emotions, letting them colour our day.

Notice also how David doesn't whitewash the challenges he faces – he names the lying enemies who seek to topple him as he looks to God for help (vv. 3–4). We too can follow David's admonition to share all that we're feeling with God: 'Pour out your hearts to him' (v. 8).

Why not pray verse 5 as a series of breath prayers today? You could inhale while praying, 'Yes, my soul' and exhale while praying, 'find rest in God'; followed by the same with 'my hope' (inhale) 'comes from him' (exhale).

Lord, in you I find my rest. My hope comes from you; I will not be shaken. Help me to trust you at all times as I pour out my heart to you. Amen
AMY BOUCHER PYE

'Lord, you're my...'

The Lord is my shepherd, I lack nothing. He makes me lie down in green pastures, he leads me beside quiet waters, he refreshes my soul. He guides me along the right paths for his name's sake. (NIV)

We end our foray into David's prayers with one of the most popular psalms ever. Psalm 23 is read out at funerals and memorised by millions; its compelling images and message continue to bring comfort and hope. We can also use it as a tool in prayer in other ways.

For instance, I love personalising Psalm 23, a simple practice of naming how God plays a multitude of roles in our lives. So as a writer I've written psalms beginning, 'The Lord is my publisher,' or perhaps my critical reviewer or editor. When I was doing academic work, I wrote renditions of the psalm as 'The Lord is my teacher,' or examiner or tutor. We could pen poems along this line of the Lord being our friend, our companion, our helper, our boss, our brother and so on. The possibilities are as individual as we are!

The Lord surely does shepherd us, leading us to rest and restoration. He guides us, leading us where we should go. In this life we will face darkness, pain and evil, but we need not fear for he promises to be with us. God prepares a feast for us to enjoy, even in the midst of our detractors. And we know that good things will follow us all our lives and that we'll live with God forever.

May you continue to join David in the Bible's prayer book as you give God your praises and pain and ask him for help and direction. Know that he loves to receive your prayers and that he's eager to meet you with a loving word or touch.

Lord, you're my life! I want to live for you; I want to give you my all. Help me always to voice my concerns and my joys to you. Thank you for your continued love and affirmation. Amen

AMY BOUCHER PYE

Paul's second letter to the Thessalonians

Mary Reid writes:

One of the best holidays my husband and I have had was a cruise entitled 'Walking in the footsteps of St Paul'. It was very moving to visit the places where Paul had started churches, to stand where he had baptised Lydia and her household (Acts 16:11–15) and see where he had been imprisoned.

We stood by the sea at Troas and were reminded of how Paul had seen, in a vision, a man begging him to come to Macedonia to help them. Paul, Silas and Timothy would have sailed in a small boat – we travelled in air-conditioned comfort across the Aegean Sea to Thessalonica.

Thessalonica is a thriving, busy seaport, and it was thriving and busy in Paul's day. He did not stay long there – on three sabbaths he went to the synagogue and began teaching about the good news of Jesus. We read in Acts 17 that there was a large crowd of Greeks and many prominent women who listened and were transformed by his message. However, there were some Jews who were jealous of Paul's success and worked up mob violence against him; so after a comparatively short stay, he had to leave and move on to Berea. Here he again went to the synagogue and taught an even larger group about Jesus. Some of the Jews in Thessalonica heard about this, went to Berea and stirred up another mob, and Paul had to move on.

Paul didn't forget them. Timothy was able to keep him informed about the difficulties the Thessalonians were facing. The gospels had not been written at this time so they only had what they could remember of Paul's teaching. They were learning to live as a loving, sharing community, but some had got confused and despondent, disagreeing about when the Lord would come again. This second letter to the Thessalonian church was therefore vital to help them cope with these complicated issues.

As we look through this short letter, written to help those first Christians to be steady in their faith in a complicated society, it could well have been written to us in 2023.

Welcome greetings

**Grace to you and peace from God our Father and the Lord Jesus Christ.
(NRSV)**

This letter is one of the earliest written by Paul. It must have been hugely
welcomed by the new young church in Thessalonica as they badly needed
some help with issues that were causing many differences of opinion
among them.

The opening greeting was exactly what they needed to read. Letters
were the only means of communication in those days and they would have
been treasured.

When did you last receive a handwritten letter from someone very special to you? Communication in the 21st century is quick and easy. We can
text someone we know living on the other side of the world. Mostly these
communications are brief, with no opening greeting, and when the subject
matter is dealt with, they are cleared. When my daughter and family lived
in America, our main means of communication was by email. They were
special so I printed off copies so I could read them again much later! Many
years ago, well before the age of the internet, I emigrated to Canada. Letters were the only means of communication, and news from home was
anxiously awaited and eagerly received.

Paul's letters would have been read and reread, discussed and prayed
about. His letters were eventually gathered up and are now part of the New
Testament, giving help and guidance to generations of Christians since.

Paul's opening greeting is as important to us today as it was then. Grace
and peace are not emotions but gifts from God himself and Jesus Christ.
In our far-from-peaceful world, we can live knowing the peace that only
God can give.

---

*Is there someone you could write to who is away from home and may need
an encouraging letter?*

MARY REID

Testing times

We must always give thanks to God for you, brothers and sisters, as is right, because your faith is growing abundantly, and the love of every one of you for one another is increasing. (NRSV)

Paul begins this letter in exactly the right way. The new Christians in Thessalonica were beginning to be full of self-doubt – they were afraid their faith was not strong enough to be tested. Yet Paul had heard good things about them, that they were a growing and loving community, and he thanked God for them. His opening words would have given them great encouragement.

They were having a difficult time as they lived in a country where the gods of Greek and Roman paganism were everywhere. Paul assured them that he constantly prayed for them and that despite the situation they lived in, the name of Jesus would be glorified (vv. 11–12).

We need to pray for Christians struggling to live in an anti-Christian environment. There are many places in the world where it is dangerous to be openly Christian.

You don't have to be living overseas to know you are not welcomed as a Christian. My first job was working in the London office of a missionary society, but once I was 18 my rail fare went up and I needed to earn a bigger salary. I moved to another job, and it didn't take long to find the jokes and conversations were very different to those overheard in the missionary society! Officially we live in a Christian country but often it doesn't seem that way.

Paul says he can boast about those new Christians in Thessalonica because of the way they behaved with love towards one another. The way we behave in our everyday life is important. We need to remember that we represent Jesus in our home, workplace, church and neighbourhood.

Dear Lord, help me to represent you in all I do and say today. Amen

MARY REID

God is in control

As to the coming of our Lord Jesus Christ and our being gathered together to him, we beg you, brothers and sisters, not to be quickly shaken in mind or alarmed. (NRSV)

This part of Paul's letter is one of the most difficult pieces of the New Testament. The Thessalonians would have understood what Paul was writing about, but we do not live with the background that they had.

Some of the new young Christians thought Paul had told them that Jesus would be returning soon, and they were nervously waiting for this great day.

Almost all the Eastern faiths believed in a power of evil. Today we have only to watch the daily newscasts or read the papers to see that we live in a time when there are many evil things happening in the world. As I write these notes, the war in Ukraine, the deepening recession and learning to live with Covid can put us into a similar state as the Thessalonian Christians.

We know that our God is in control of all that is happening in our world. We are encouraged to pray for every situation and for those in need. We know that it is God's world, and he will have the final say.

Over the years, there have been Christians who have tried to work out the actual date of the second coming and have gathered on Mount Sinai ready to meet with the Lord. And nothing has ever happened! Jesus said that no one knows the day and time but God the Father (Mark 13:32). What we can be certain of is that all those who love the Lord will be there.

In the meantime, we live in a time when evil exists, but the Holy Spirit is with us in our everyday life. We can't sort out everything that is wrong in our world, but we can bring the love of Jesus to those we live and work with each day.

Pray for someone you know who is in real need today and thank God for something you hear that has helped others.

MARY REID

Hold fast

So then, brothers and sisters, stand firm and hold fast to the traditions that you were taught by us, either by word of mouth or by our letter. (NRSV)

Paul knew that learning to live as Christians in Thessalonian society was going to be difficult, and his advice to them was to stand firm and hold fast to everything they had so far heard about Jesus and God the Father. They had to remember what he had taught them.

We probably have more than one copy of the Bible in our possession, but we don't always carry one with us every day. It is as important for us to really know what we believe as it was for those early Christians.

As a teenager, I was given a small set of cards with important Bible quotations, plus references, to learn by heart. As I find learning anything by rote difficult, I was not too keen on them at the time, but as all my friends were using them, I persisted – and how glad I am now that I did. Over the years those texts have often come to mind just when I needed to know what to do or say as a Christian.

The words of hymns, too, can stick in the mind. In the 18th century, when John Newton, initially a slave trader, was converted he became a parish priest in Olney in Buckinghamshire. He was joined by William Cowper, a poet, and between them they wrote hymns for the parishioners, mostly uneducated silk workers. These people probably worked long hours and would doze off during sermons. Teaching them to sing gospel hymns was a brilliant idea. The words from hymns that we have sung for years help us in our everyday life to stand firm and hold fast to our faith.

Thank God for those who have helped you in your growth as a Christian.

MARY REID

Pray for us

Finally, brothers and sisters, pray for us, so that the word of the Lord may spread rapidly and be glorified everywhere. (NRSV)

Paul often faced opposition and violence (v. 2). He needed the Christians in Thessalonica to pray for his protection from those who opposed the gospel.

This still happens today. Not everyone who hears the gospel preached believes and can end up in opposition causing as much trouble as possible. We need to pray for our church leaders – they may not suffer the violent opposition that Paul experienced, but many smaller things can go wrong in a local church that make it difficult for the gospel to be spread in the community.

Prayer support is so important for every Christian working to take the love of God to others. Most missionary societies produce literature that gives information about their work and who to pray for each day. My husband once met an elderly, housebound woman who made it her life's work to pray for a different part of the world every day. She had collected information from many different societies, and on the table in front of her she laid out the appropriate leaflets about the area of the world she was praying for that day. She would never be able to meet these people, but she prayed for them by name, and for their needs. Hers was a truly important ministry.

We don't always have to be on our knees in a quiet place to pray. When my children were at the demanding preschool age, finding somewhere quiet to pray was difficult. Eventually, I found a small book with verses to read for every day of the year. I kept it on the bedroom windowsill so I could read it while the children thought I was making the beds, and it gave me ideas about what to pray for in the spaces of the day. Many years later this was exactly what *Day by Day with God* was produced for, to help busy women know what to pray for each day.

Spend time today praying for your church leaders as they seek to make Jesus known in your community.

MARY REID

An example to follow

Brothers and sisters, do not be weary in doing what is right. (NRSV)

How often do you hear that volunteers are needed in your church or community? I must admit that my reaction is not always good – I'm already too busy/too old/not gifted in that area!

Here Paul has heard that some of his new believers were so excited at the prospect of the second coming that they had given up any work and were 'living in idleness'. 'Anyone unwilling to work should not eat', writes Paul (v. 10). The Jewish law insisted that a trained Rabbi, as Paul was, should take no pay for his teaching but must have an honest trade. Paul was a tentmaker, and he worked day and night at this trade as an example for others to follow.

All too often in churches, and other organisations, there are people who take on the responsibility of running everything and many more who are happy to sit back and do nothing! One church I belonged to in Canada expected everyone to be involved in something to help in the running of the church. If you took on a major responsibility, you only did it for one year, then stood down and did a less time-consuming job, like delivering a few magazines. This worked very well, and I was impressed and tried to encourage this back in my home church.

There are always people who have gladly taken on a regular responsibility in the running of their church – from leading a weekly women's group to dealing with refreshments whenever needed. In a loving, caring church, others should make sure this work is shared to ensure those taking on such commitments have plenty of help and support. Paul urges us not to be weary in doing what is right – perhaps it would be good to reassess your use of time.

Are you involved too little, or too much, in your church community?

MARY REID

Peace be with you

Now may the Lord of peace himself give you peace at all times in all ways. (NRSV)

Right at the end of this short letter, Paul has some stern things to say to those who are causing trouble in the church (vv. 14–15). He is quite fierce, saying they must have nothing to do with troublemakers.

I know of one church where the congregation was completely split in two. One side was against the minister and the other side was completely for him. The argument had started between two people with different opinions, and then others had taken sides. Paul's advice was very much needed here – no one should take sides. The original troublemakers should have been left on their own until they felt ashamed of themselves.

However, all problems within church family need to be dealt with in a loving way. Having nothing to do with troublemakers doesn't mean they are judged as enemies – they are still our brothers and sisters in Christ. Forgiveness is a necessary ingredient and will ensure all problems are dealt with in love.

The Thessalonian church may have received letters 'from Paul' that were actually from someone else. This could have been why some of the believers were expecting Jesus to come back to them very soon. Another person may well have put his own opinion about the second coming in a letter and to give it authority had signed it as from Paul. Paul may well have realised this had happened and was the cause of all the trouble and confusion among the believers. Paul would have dictated his own letters to a scribe, so he ends this letter with his own signature, pointing out that his readers must learn to recognise the way he writes his name.

In his final words to them, he wishes them peace and grace, both gifts they needed in that early young church and gifts that we so much need today.

Dear Lord, help me to know your peace and grace today. Amen

MARY REID

Prepare the way

Jackie Harris writes:

I have lost count of the times people have said to me recently: 'Where has the time gone?' Certainly, Christmas seems to come round increasingly quickly – not helped by Christmas cards, mince pies and Christmas decorations appearing in some shops in September!

But before we reach Christmas, there is Advent, the beginning of the ecclesiastical year and a time for reflection and prayer before the big celebration. In this season, we remember Jesus' coming as a baby to fulfil God's promises to the people of Israel and we look forward to Jesus' second coming, when he will return in glory to restore all things.

As I pondered the meaning of Advent, I was reminded of a play by Daphne du Maurier – *The Years Between* – which I first read many years ago. Its title struck a chord as I thought about Jesus' first coming and the promised second coming. We are living in the years between those two great events. How then should we live? What should be our priorities? How can we help to prepare the way for others to recognise the Saviour of the world?

I'm indebted to the contributors in this issue and to some guest contributors from our team of writers who help us to think through some of these questions. A couple of our contributors look back to the funeral of Queen Elizabeth II last year. It was a pivotal moment when faith was put centre stage and openly discussed. I wonder how many people have begun searching for Jesus as a result of that final witness.

Paul, in his letter to the Romans, says: 'Our salvation is nearer now than when we first believed' (13:11, NIV). Let's use this Advent season to consider how we might use the time we have in these in-between years.

Stay in the light

If we walk in the light as he himself is in the light, we have fellowship with one another. (NRSV)

John wrote this letter before he was exiled to Patmos (Revelation 1:9). Jerusalem had been destroyed in AD70 and more than one generation of Christians had faced severe persecution. Those who had survived were beginning to conform to the standards of the people around them.

John's letter was to remind Christians that God is light, he is perfectly holy and true, and Christians are meant to live out their lives in this light. Jesus himself said: 'You are the light of the world' (Matthew 5:14). We reflect this light to the world we live in – it is not simply a sentimental, emotional love but a dynamic love that offers help to those around us.

In the small town where I live, there are many who need help: people struggling to cope with the rise in the cost of living who rely on our food banks; elderly people living alone who are afraid to go to the supermarket after the Covid pandemic; and children who need a meal during school holidays. There are many who willingly give time to meet these needs – not only Christians. At the same time, the church is seeing a drop in the number of people who come to church every Sunday.

The problem is that Sunday is no longer a day of rest; most shops are open, children's sports clubs often happen on Sunday mornings and, when the sun is shining, it is very tempting to spend the day on the nearest beach! Before we know it, our Sunday worship is reduced to a monthly event.

It is easy to find that we are conforming to the world around us and gradually losing the light of God. Meeting, worshipping and praying with one another is vital. In this time of Advent, let's make sure we make fellowship with one another a priority.

Pray about your commitments over the coming weeks, remembering that we are called out of darkness into his marvellous light (1 Peter 2:9).

MARY REID

Slow down

'Here is your God!' See, the Sovereign Lord comes with power, and he rules with a mighty arm. See, his reward is with him, and his recompense accompanies him. He tends his flock like a shepherd. (NIV)

Isaiah 40 speaks of one who will come, the one for whom John the Baptist is called to prepare the way (Matthew 3:3). The one who is promised will be powerful; it is the Lord himself! And yet, he is gentle. He is the shepherd of the sheep. We may remember here the words of Jesus in John 10:11, describing himself as the 'good shepherd' who 'lays down his life for the sheep'.

Jesus was born in humble circumstances, not in a palace. He came as a servant, to 'give his life as a ransom for many' (Matthew 20:28). He died on a cross and was buried in a borrowed tomb. This is our king. He is the Most High and yet, as we welcome him, we are also welcoming the one who washes his disciples' feet (John 13:5).

So often during this busy period, when we are rushing around buying gifts, preparing food and meeting friends and family, we can easily forget to stop and listen for the voice of our gentle shepherd. We may feel as if we simply don't have time to wait and reflect on just who it is we are celebrating at Christmas!

As we make our preparations, we need to ensure that our focus is on the one who tells us that in essence, there is only one important thing – and that is to spend time with him (Luke 10:38–42). It may take some real discipline, and even thoughtful planning, but let's remember to take time out to prepare our hearts to receive our loving king, and not let the world and all its worries drive us from his presence.

Lord, in the busyness of this season, help me to remember that it's all about you! Amen

SHEILA JACOBS

Be a faithful witness

Thomas said… 'How can we know the way?' Jesus answered, 'I am the way and the truth and the life. No one comes to the Father except through me. If you really know me, you will know my Father as well. From now on, you do know him and have seen him.' (NIV)

How do you prepare the way for someone who *is* the way? Before reading on, read the passage again and ask yourself that question.

Advent is often seen as a time of preparing our hearts for the birth of Jesus – many find this helpful within the rhythm of the church's year. But is Jesus reborn in us each day as the carol 'O little town of Bethlehem' implies, or indeed each year, at Christmastime? No. Since the resurrection, Jesus has stayed alive, but he keeps on refreshing and renewing our hope, faith and love.

Those yet to meet or follow Jesus are, effectively, lost. How can we prepare their path to Jesus? 'Come and see,' said Philip to Nathanael (John 1:46). We can't always make that personal introduction, but we can show something of Jesus through the way we live – for example, as we obey his commands, love and trust him and allow the Holy Spirit to give us his wisdom and peace, even in difficult times.

Watching the funeral of Queen Elizabeth II last year, I was struck by the way her life, along with a few well-chosen words, demonstrated the way to follow Jesus. Her steadfastness in fulfilling a calling not of her choosing, her extraordinary humility, patience, service, quiet wisdom, interest in and concern for others, even when going through horrible times herself – these virtues, so undervalued in our culture, shone brighter than any jewel she wore. Even cynical, critical commentators saw that she drew strength over so many decades from her faith in Jesus – who is the way, the truth and the fullness of life eternal.

Lord, may we all seek your help to live your way wherever you have placed us. Help us to be faithful witnesses to those around us. Amen

CHRIS LEONARD

Pray the Lord's Prayer

'**Our Father in heaven, hallowed be your name, your kingdom come, your will be done, on earth as it is in heaven.**' (NIV)

These familiar words from the Lord's Prayer are particularly pertinent as we think about preparing for the Lord's coming. Let's consider each phrase and how it might inspire our prayers in this Advent season.

We begin, 'Our Father', reminding ourselves not only that we pray to someone who loves and understands us, but also that we are called to pray for others.

'Hallowed be your name' leads us to consider all that God is and perhaps some of the many names for, or descriptions of, God in the Bible. We might like to ask that God would reveal himself to us as our shepherd, provider, protector or healer. And remembering that we pray 'Our Father', we can pray in the same way for others who we know to be in need.

'Your kingdom come' reminds us that prayer is not about presenting a list of requests or asking God's blessing on our plans, but rather seeking to understand what God wants us to do. How might he want to shape our lives? What is on his heart for the communities of which we are a part?

'Your will be done' is a prayer of submission. It encourages us to bring our hopes and ambitions, or indeed our frustrations, fears or difficulties, before him, praying as Jesus did in the garden of Gethsemane: 'Not my will, but yours be done' (Luke 22:42).

As we continue in prayer, we are encouraged to ask God for what we (and others) need each day, to confess our sins and to think about our dealings with others. Finally, we pray for God's protection. I find *The Message* translation helpful here: 'Keep us safe from ourselves and the Devil.' We ask that God would keep us close and enable us to resist anything that would seek to draw us away from his truth.

Based on an article included in *Prayer: A Christian companion*, edited by Susan Hibbins (Inspire, 2006).

Pray the Lord's Prayer each day from now until Christmas, perhaps concentrating on a different word or phrase each day to inspire your prayers and help keep you focused on the wonder of God with us.

JACKIE HARRIS

As we wait

The one who calls you is faithful, and he will do this. (NRSV)

At my theological college, a bell was rung to call us to services. It was a tricky task on dark winter mornings, keeping an eye on one's watch and ringing the bell at the right time. Many in the college community relied on the bell to make it to prayers on time, so I always felt a weight of responsibility when it was my turn. There's an inscription on the bell – words from 1 Thessalonians 5:24 – 'The one who calls you is faithful.' A fabulous reminder on wobbly days for those of us training for church ministry. In fact, a fabulous reminder for any Christian, on all sorts of days – both good and bad – particularly when we are on the brink of something new.

God calls us into new seasons of life, new experiences of faith, new ways of being. The passage we read today is full of advice for living a life in expectation of the change to come. No one knows when the day of the Lord will be – which I find an interesting paradox in this season of the year. We prepare now for the birth of Christ, even as we are waiting for his return to come.

What does this life look like? One lived with faith, love and the hope of salvation. One where we inspire each other to hold fast to what is good. One where we are people of peace and patience. One where we give thanks in all circumstances. Some things on this list are rather easier than others, aren't they? This letter encourages us to discipled, disciplined life today. We may have one eye on the future, but if we follow even a small part of the instructions today, we will reflect the light of Christ to the lives of those around us.

Lord, I strive to pray without ceasing and to rejoice always, but I don't always manage it! Help me find words of thankfulness in whatever circumstances I ind myself in today. Amen

SARA BATTS-NEALE

Make room for Jesus

'A voice of one calling in the wilderness, "Prepare the way for the Lord, make straight paths for him. Every valley shall be filled in, every mountain and hill made low. The crooked roads shall become straight, the rough ways smooth. And all people will see God's salvation."' (NIV)

This was John's time to fulfil the calling that had been spoken over him before conception and at the time of his circumcision – to prepare the way for Jesus. Like many Old Testament prophets before him, John stood out as an unusual character (he wore camel's hair and ate locusts, while living out in the wilderness – see Matthew 3:1–12). Yet people travelled to hear him regardless of his appearance, even wondering if he was the messiah.

John was very clear in his identity and was at pains to point out that he was not worthy in comparison to the one he was announcing. This was not false humility or low self-esteem. John was confident in what he was called to do (share the good news of the one coming and baptise people as a sign of repentance), while recognising and honouring the worth of Jesus.

At this time of year, we can find ourselves bombarded with feelings of inadequacy as we seek to juggle myriad different plates in order to prepare for 'the perfect Christmas' – whatever that is. While our culture may expect us to work, bake endless Christmas goodies, decorate our homes beautifully and find the best presents for our families, this is not what Jesus requires of us.

Take a moment now just to pause and think about whether you have allowed yourself to get caught up in our culture's ideal Christmas. Jesus is actually longing for you to pause and prepare your own heart afresh for him this Christmas. As you do that, he can work in and through you. Then, as you go about your daily life, be aware that you may well be preparing the way for others to see a glimpse of the real Christmas truth too.

Take some time to sit before Jesus and offer him your heart. Then ask him to lead you as you prepare the way for not only yourself, but also those around you too, to get a glimpse of him this Christmas.

CLAIRE MUSTERS

Strength for the day

Yet I will rejoice in the Lord, I will be joyful in God my Saviour. The Sovereign Lord is my strength. (NIV)

There are times in my life when I have become so overwhelmed with the state of the world that I have had to take a break from reading or listening to the news. This is particularly true since I became a mother. The weight of the world seems to rest heavy on my shoulders, and I fear for my children and their future.

The world can be a scary place. We hear of wars and rumours of wars, of dictators and despots, and of climate change that threatens the very existence of our planet. It sometimes seems like the darkness is overcoming the light – that violence, corruption and hatred are more prevalent than goodness and kindness.

The prophet Habakkuk lived in a time of uncertainty for God's people as they awaited battle with the Babylonians. Earlier in the book, after complaining to God about the wickedness he sees around him and asking for Judah to be spared, the prophet writes of positioning himself on the ramparts to watch and await God's answer (2:1). This image reminds me that we need to take a long view of history and remind ourselves of what God has done before.

In today's reading, after Habakkuk reminds himself of who God is and of his sovereign power, he chooses to trust in the everlasting God rather than being affected by all that he sees around him. He is watching and waiting for the day of calamity but still clinging on to hope.

When we are facing times of difficulty and tragedy in our own lives, or wincing at headlines warning of doom, we too can choose to put our trust in a sovereign God. Like Habakkuk, we will find a Saviour God who gives us the strength to face each new day, no matter what may come our way.

Sovereign God, we thank you that you remain the same yesterday, today and forever. Thank you that you are not fazed by anything. Help us to look up to you and choose to trust in the God who never leaves us or forsakes us. Amen
CHINE MCDONALD

Our security is in God

For thus says the high and lofty one who inhabits eternity, whose name is Holy; I dwell in the high and holy place, and also with those who are contrite and humble in spirit. (NRSV)

In Isaiah's time, the people were turning to pagan gods to ensure their security. They went up to the high places (v. 7) and down to the low places of the valley where they had sexual orgies and killed their own children as sacrifices (vv. 5–6). High and low. In both locations, their worship was wrong because it was to the wrong gods (prosperity and fertility) and in the wrong way (through pleasure and destruction).

In contrast, Isaiah describes true worship by making a play on the 'high and low' concept. God is in a high place (v. 15), but spiritually, not geographically. God's loftiness is to do with his character and holiness, which surpasses any goodness we can imagine. God is above our ways, and this is good news. Crucially, it does not make God remote. God is with the lowly in spirit. The great secret for preparing the way of the Lord (v. 14) is humility and contrition. It's not about what is seen and displayed, but what is inside our character and spirit. Hence John the Baptist preached repentance and humility before Christ's first coming, and it's how we need to prepare for Christ's second coming, whenever that may be.

In practical terms, it means we should look to God, not money, romance or power, for our security in life. It means our worship should not involve self-deprivation nor self-gratification. It's not about being centre stage in our church or lives, but being humble before God, who is both high in heaven and low alongside us. God comes near to the humble. What does that mean for us? It means recognising our frailty, our limitations, our failings. It means not hiding them but looking up to God. May we begin that transformation today.

Holy God, forgive us for looking for our security in the wrong places. Forgive us for viewing ourselves wrongly. Come, Lord Jesus. May we prepare the way by living humble lives that honour you and the people around us. Amen

TANYA MARLOW

Sing God's praise

About midnight Paul and Silas were praying and singing hymns to God, and the other prisoners were listening to them. (NIV)

Preparation carries the connotation of hard work. I've got twelve family members here for a birthday dinner in a couple of days, so I'm thinking all about the menu and shopping, making beds and cleaning bathrooms. The challenge is not to get the work done, but to get it done with the right attitude – an attitude of gratitude that we can all gather for a celebration.

Paul and Silas had been stripped, badly beaten, put into an inner (dark) cell and tethered in stocks. Rather than complaining or even pleading to God for release, they raised their voices in praise. Under such severe testing, their startling focus on the glory of God amazed fellow prisoners and had a supernatural effect. It shook the foundations of the prison and led to the jailer and his whole household accepting Jesus as Lord.

I first encountered God in a personal, relational way when standing among a group of believers who were praising Jesus with their whole hearts. Their praise had power to remove my fears and doubts, and the King of glory entered in.

Scripture is filled with examples of the power of praise. When believers align their beings with God, lost in wonder and adoration, the enemy is rendered powerless. Believers are refreshed as God is revealed through them.

In this study, focusing on preparing the way of the Lord, we can become enmeshed in serious prayer to remove obstacles we perceive to be preventing others or ourselves from receiving Jesus. I am not discounting a need for sober prayer and fasting, but I believe the default attitude and first action in preparing the way for relationship with God is praise.

Praise is a recognition that God is in charge. It lifts the burden of responsibility from us. Hallelujah!

Use Psalm 150 to set the stage for your praise. Sing out your praise to God, who so loved the world that he came to dwell among us. Rejoice in the truth of the Christmas message.

MICHELE D. MORRISON

What are you wearing?

And over all these virtues put on love, which binds them all together in perfect unity. (NIV)

How do we prepare to celebrate the coming of Christ? When Paul wrote to the Christians in Colossae, he didn't have Advent in mind. But the way of life which he urged Christians to follow stands out as a great model for us during Advent today.

Do we show the characteristics that Paul says should mark us out as those God loves: compassion, kindness, humility, gentleness and patience? They sound easy enough, but we don't show these things automatically. We're often grumpy, mean, self-centred, rude and impatient. Paul talks about us 'clothing' ourselves with better qualities. We put them on, cover up our inadequacies, become kinder, gentler and more compassionate people. Once we're wearing this layer, the next set of clothes fits better: forgiveness, peace, gratitude. Then love ties everything together. This kind of clothing comes with Holy Spirit-living; when we put it on, we bless everyone around us. Choosing our clothes carefully is great Advent preparation.

Paul's focus is on the whole Christian community. We share these characteristics in our relationships with each other and in worship. Whether we're singing, teaching, admonishing or praying, we do it in thankfulness to God and anticipation of God's great gift in Jesus. We're also to be watchful – a great Advent word – looking beyond Christian community for opportunities God gives us to share the gospel. We guard our relationships with outsiders, being both wise and gracious in how we treat them. We support those who are sharing the gospel elsewhere, often in places far from home, especially praying for those suffering persecution or imprisonment (like Paul himself).

Does this sound like your church this Advent? If not, can you be the one who asks God to help you to encourage others so you're ready and waiting for Christ's coming?

Lord, we thank you that you give the Holy Spirit to those who ask. We pray that your Spirit will guide us through this Advent and get our hearts ready to receive Jesus. Amen

ELAINE STORKEY

Hear, receive, obey

Do not merely listen to the word, and so deceive yourselves. Do what it says. (NIV)

Sometimes when we're out walking, my dog gets distracted by a particularly interesting smell and ends up lagging behind with her nose in the grass. I'll call her name and whistle for her to come to heel. She'll look up, spot me, and then go right back to sniffing. She is a perfect example of one who hears a word of instruction but does not do what it says.

Do you ever have those dog-sniff moments? James says we all do. In this passage, he is reminding us that we need to be quick to listen and obey. To just listen and then go right back to sniffing (as it were) is to deceive yourself.

But there's more. James is also instructing his readers to be slow to speak and slow to become angry. Any Christian who finds themselves in a heated argument should, first and foremost, seek to listen rather than respond.

This feels like basic advice, doesn't it? Listen to understand, not to reply. Don't get cross unnecessarily. That's not to say we shouldn't become angry at the things that deserve it – injustice, abuse, inequality – but on a daily basis, it's likely that our anger is more about wounded pride than right and wrong behaviour in God's sight. And our anger is often misdirected – coming out in snapped words and passive-aggressive actions, rather than being brought to Jesus and left with him.

And so, we come full circle – don't just listen to God's instructions to be slow to speak and slow to anger. Don't just acknowledge them as good advice and then – like my Labrador – proceed to ignore them. As we prepare our hearts to receive Jesus, we need not only to hear, but also to receive and obey as well.

Hear, receive, obey – no matter how good the distracting smell might be.

A version of this article first appeared on **licc.org.uk**

Father God, give me the courage and the integrity not just to hear your words, but also to receive them and obey them too. May I be slow to speak and slow to anger this week. Amen

ALIANORE SMITH

Be a sweet scent

For we are to God the pleasing aroma of Christ among those who are being saved and those who are perishing. To the one we are an aroma that brings death; to the other, an aroma that brings life. (NIV)

Covid-19 didn't affect my sense of taste or smell, but for some people afflicted with this disease, altered senses mean that things they used to enjoy – such as coffee – now seem disgustingly medicinal. This side effect starkly divides their life from before to after Covid.

The apostle Paul draws a strong image of an aroma dividing those who follow Christ and those who reject him. He is writing to the church at Corinth, addressing those who questioned his ministry and why he didn't come to visit them as he had anticipated he would. He shares how in following God, sometimes our plans change (2 Corinthians 2:12–13). Even so, those who follow Christ 'spread the aroma of the knowledge of him everywhere' (v. 14). Sometimes this aroma is pleasing and sometimes sour; to those who follow Christ, we are like a sweet scent, but we can smell foul to those who do not.

I wonder if we sometimes forget or disregard this divisive nature of serving Christ – that some will reject us because of our faith. In our culture, we like to emphasise acceptance and inclusion – and rightly so. But God also calls us to preach the gospel in all of its richness and fullness, meaning that we can't water down the demands he makes for Christians to love him first and foremost. We can be winsome in our speech and in our actions, but we also have to be true to the message of Christ.

May we be those who show their love to others in gracious and compelling ways, that our lives would emit an intriguing and sweet smell that leads others to Christ.

Gracious God, make us ready to share your love and truth with grace and peace. Through the Holy Spirit, may we be an aroma that brings life. Amen
AMY BOUCHER PYE

The road home

People of Israel, you are my own dear children. Don't I love you best of all? Though I often make threats, I want you to be near me, so I will have mercy on you. I, the Lord, have spoken. With rock piles and signposts, mark the road well, my dear people. The road by which you left by will now lead you home. (CEV)

A state funeral. Wide London streets lined with people from all walks of life, many of whom had queued all night in the cold and rain to pay their respects and to demonstrate their love as a coffin was pulled slowly through the streets. Watched by millions on TV, the funeral of Queen Elizabeth II in September 2022 was executed with reverence, while brimming with dazzling pomp and ceremony. Talk about preparing the way – it was an organisational triumph! It represented, but maybe almost obscured, the quieter, shorter, simpler journey surely already taken by our monarch at her moment of death. A familiar road – one she had been travelling on all her life – the road home.

It's a journey that can only ever be taken alone. Prepared for each of us at our birth, it's a journey full of possibilities – of being lured into ditches or on to tracks that lead nowhere, of being blinded by fierce sun, lost in periods of dense fog or having our vision obscured by driving rain. But it is also a journey with the never-wavering promise that if we choose, we can be guided back on to a familiar ancient road that we recognise as the right one. Maybe that too is an organisational triumph involving goodness knows how many guardian angels under the authority of the Holy Spirit, the last few miles lit by spiritual cats-eyes leading us towards the safety of a triune God who is not willing that any should be lost.

We will soon be celebrating the birth of Jesus, whose human journey home also involved having to resist being lured from the path chosen for him. Crucially, at moments of greatest temptation, he refused to take advantage of his royal privileges to avoid obstacles or to jump the queue on his way to suffering, success and home.

Father, we're sorry for when we have felt, as your royal children, that we should somehow be entitled to an easier path through life. Thank you, Jesus, for never giving in, and thank you for never giving up on us. Amen

BRIDGET PLASS

Keep your lamp burning

All the bridesmaids got up and prepared their lamps. Then the five foolish ones asked the others, 'Please give us some of your oil because our lamps are going out.' (NLT)

Advent is a glorious time of anticipation and preparation for the celebration of Jesus' birth. But it can also be a time of exhaustion and of sadness that our plans or hopes for the year haven't quite happened. With depleted spiritual, physical and emotional resources, we too, like five of the bridesmaids, can feel that our lamps are about to go out!

The ten bridesmaids had much to anticipate. They were waiting for the arrival of the bridegroom, which often took place at night, so each had their lamp. As they waited, they all became drowsy and fell asleep. When the bridegroom finally arrived, five of them faced the awful realisation that they had run out of oil – they'd failed to prepare for the unexpected and missed his return.

As I read this familiar passage, I began to wonder about my 'lamp' – not only in terms of my readiness and preparation for Jesus' return, but also how my life might be the light Jesus declared it to be (Matthew 5:14–16).

Your 'lamp' may be different in shape and style to mine; mine seems battered and misshaped as life has taken its toll. What matters more, though, than its external state is the light within. Sometimes it burns brightly. Other times there's barely a flicker as the challenges and concerns of life conspire to extinguish it. Yet somehow that hope within continues to burn.

The Holy Spirit is the oil that fills our lives. Spending time in prayer and reading God's word keeps our lamps burning. Sharing in Communion and fellowship with others fan the flames as we encourage and pray for one another, not only in preparing for Jesus' return, but also to help others find their way to him.

Advent is a time filled with lights burning brightly. Let our lives burn brighter still.

God of hope, please keep pouring your oil on to that flame within us so that we can shine brightly for you, now and always. Amen

SANDRA WHEATLEY

The Christmas story

Elaine Storkey writes:

Every year it feels as if the gap widens a little more between the culture's narrative of Christmas and the Bible's narrative. It's not just that the Advent season is crowded out by glitzy shopping centres and endless advertising, but Christmas itself can bring anxiety as the cost of presents, food, travel and family needs takes its toll. The reality of the incarnation can seem far away as working mums struggle to get everything ready in time and divided families wonder how they can get through it while keeping the children happy.

I find it a huge relief to turn from our culture's view of Christmas to the nativity story in the Bible. There's nothing drab or wearying in this narrative. It's intricate and exciting, full of diverse characters whose ordinary lives experience extraordinary events. And it is all set dramatically against the backcloth of a turbulent time in real history. For the Christ child comes into a world dominated by geo-politics and the power of imperial rule.

Everyone in the text has a story to tell: Elizabeth and Mary, both chosen by God for special pregnancies; Zechariah and Joseph, their menfolk who play a supportive, if subsidiary, role; the long list of ancestors; the foetus leaping in its mother's womb; the shepherds whose night shift is interrupted by singing angels; the faithful elderly prophets who have waited a lifetime for this event. We hear from them all and they pack the narrative with amazing detail. Nothing is incidental: a naming ceremony, a visit to the temple, the long journey of distant Eastern sages or the anger of a ruthless king; everything is significant. It all fits together as the biblical authors, inspired by God, share with us the greatest story ever told.

Those who love the scriptures know much about Christ coming to be one of us. I hope these new reflections will shape the way we approach this wonderful season and help us celebrate with joy and depth. But the New Testament looks forward as well as back. With the upheaval of life today and the issues surrounding us in our world, it seems appropriate to reflect on what we know less about – Jesus' coming again. We end this year with the final sequel to the nativity story, the second coming of Christ. May God's Spirit help us live in readiness for that.

A woman's worth

'The Lord has done this for me,' she said. 'In these days he has shown his favour and taken away my disgrace among the people.' (NIV)

Two women are involved in the nativity story. They are cousins from an impeccable Jewish line but beyond that their differences are obvious. One is old and has no children; the other is young and has no husband. Yet the God of miracles is at work in them both. They will each become pregnant and receive the miraculous gift of new birth.

Luke tells Elizabeth's story first. We find that although she is a God-fearing, upright woman and a faithful wife, she sees herself as inadequate. It's unsurprising given the culture of the day. A married woman who has produced no heirs to continue her husband's line is viewed as something of a disgrace to the family. Her husband Zechariah continues to pray for her, yet when the angel tells him his prayers have been heard and his aged wife will become pregnant and bear a son, his response reveals a lack of faith. Again, this is unsurprising though; he won't be under any illusion about their current ability to procreate! Being robbed of speech doesn't help his communication with Elizabeth, but with such powerful changes in her body it isn't long before she grasps what's happening. Retreating into seclusion, she can reflect on the miracle God is producing in her.

I love the way Elizabeth takes it personally: 'The Lord has done this for me.' She no longer sees herself as an ineffective old woman, shut out from other women's experiences and dismissed as inadequate. In reality, this was never who she was. It's not how God sees any one of us. It took a miraculous pregnancy for Elizabeth to understand how well God knows and loves her. Whatever our situation, let's receive God's love now for ourselves, and thrive in its warmth.

Thank you, God, that you see through the values and attitudes of our culture, and that you invite us to see ourselves not through the distorted lens they offer but through the kindness and acceptance of your love. Amen

ELAINE STORKEY

Responding to the angel

The angel said to her, 'Do not be afraid, Mary, you have found favour with God. You will conceive and give birth to a son, and you are to call him Jesus. He will be great and will be called the Son of the Most High.' (NIV)

The angels are having a busy time. Now it's Mary's turn to receive the extraordinary news that she is to become pregnant. This is not just on a par with her elderly cousin's late pregnancy; it's an entirely bigger dimension. The angel's news of the miraculous conception of her future offspring must have sounded overwhelming to Mary. She was hearing that she herself would bring the long-awaited Messiah, the anointed one, into the world.

Mary's only question concerns her own role. She's not in any sexual relationship. What about the small question of a husband? Could she really be part of God's plan? The angel's explanation of a miraculous conception must have sounded incredible, even unbelievable, yet Mary accepts it completely. Her spirit is in tune with the Holy Spirit of God, and she puts herself without reserve at God's service.

However, God's service is not always straightforward. For Mary, it will bring misunderstanding and ostracism, requiring an angelic visit to Joseph to reassure him of her faithfulness. She will be warned by old Simeon that her heart will be broken ('a sword will pierce your own soul' – Luke 2:35). She will stand at the cross and watch her precious son die.

God's call on us might take us into many situations we find it hard to cope with. It might sometimes bring us sorrow and pain. But that is the nature of discipleship in a broken world. It doesn't mean God has let us down, or we've got things wrong. It just means we're in a season of trial and hardship which requires yet more faith and hope. Trusting God is a lifetime occupation. But we can take it on with the help of the Holy Spirit. Whatever we face, God will continue to uphold us and give us the strength to go on.

Heavenly Father, help me to hear you when you call me to something beyond my normal comfort zone. Please give me the confidence that your power is enough to enable me to see it through. Amen

ELAINE STORKEY

Cousins sharing miracles

When Elizabeth heard Mary's greeting, the baby leaped in her womb, and Elizabeth was filled with the Holy Spirit. In a loud voice she exclaimed: 'Blessed are you among women, and blessed is the child you will bear!' (NIV)

Those of us who grew up with cousins know something of the ties that bind us. My closest cousin in age was my best friend throughout childhood and it was a joy to share experiences of pregnancy years later. So, it was unremarkable that pregnant Mary should want to see her older cousin and make the arduous journey to her home. Yet what happened as they met took them both by surprise. Elizabeth could hardly believe the powerful reaction of the foetus in her womb to the sound of Mary's voice. She realised that the unborn baby John recognised, even while in the cocoon of his mother's body, that his Saviour was present before him, and he leapt with joy.

The baby's reaction was followed by both cousins being filled with the Holy Spirit and pouring out praise and blessings. The wonderful prophetic song we call the Magnificat is Mary joining her voice with the prophets of the Hebrew scriptures to recount God's faithfulness to his people. God will bring down the mighty and proud, elevate the meek and humble and find food for the hungry. And to do this, God will often use those people the world regards as of no consequence. Mary, young and insignificant, was to be both the prophet proclaiming God's liberating power and the mother of God's Son.

This authentic outpouring of praise from the cousins is a reminder that God has used women in his plan of redemption throughout the ages. He has called so many of us into serving, teaching and healing, as well as into advocacy for those who have no voices. As we sing Mary's song with her, we can ask afresh that the Holy Spirit might deepen in us the compassion of God for those in need and equip us today to be God's effective servants.

Think of the women who have inspired you as a Christian. What is it about their character or lives that has brought you closer to understanding and experiencing the love of God?

ELAINE STORKEY

What's in a name?

On the eighth day they came to circumcise the child, and they were going to name him after his father Zechariah, but his mother spoke up and said, 'No! He is to be called John.' (NIV)

Travelling in India, I was invited to an exuberant neighbourhood celebration after the birth of a boy. (I found out afterwards that this would not have happened for a baby girl.) So, to a degree, I can envisage the birth festivities for Elizabeth's son; circumcision (cutting the foreskin of the penis) was then a traditional health and identity ritual. However, the naming process caused confusion. Elizabeth's insistence that her baby should be called 'John' rather than given his father's name didn't fit family expectations. Yet the name given by an angel should surely supersede cultural traditions. When Zechariah had the last word (it was a patriarchal society!) and confirmed in writing that the name should indeed be John, a double celebration followed. Agreeing with the angel and Elizabeth wonderfully unlocked his power of speech.

Names are important as identifiers. John's name means 'God is gracious'. It signified that he had been called by God for a special ministry to proclaim the Messiah's coming. His name was a constant reminder of God's mercy and graciousness to people far and wide. They called him 'the Baptist' too because those who heeded his warnings and repented of their sins were baptised by him.

Our names are also important. They're a crucial part of our identity, carrying deep personal connections that sometimes go back generations. Whenever someone remembers our name and treats it with respect, we feel accepted and affirmed. If we hear our name slandered it hurts. I've also met people who have received a new name from God, which has brought healing from pain in the past. We can joyfully share what God told Israel: 'I have redeemed you; I have called you by name, you are mine' (Isaiah 43:1 ESV). God knows our name, and in his love we will always have significance.

Father God, we thank you that you know us through and through, and that our names are engraved on the palms of your hand. Please help us to build up our identity in you, so that in our lives people will see Jesus. Amen

ELAINE STORKEY

Prophecy and obedience

'You will go on before the Lord to prepare the way for him, to give his people the knowledge of salvation through the forgiveness of their sins.' (NIV)

Elizabeth understood that the order of birth was significant. Her son would be the one who went ahead of Mary's son, to prepare his way. John's leap in his mother's womb was one of anticipation. He would be a 'prophet of the Most High' (v . 76). He would live a life of obedience, fulfilling the prophecy that his father Zechariah spoke over him in the power of the Holy Spirit. And the church would echo Zechariah's song in worship, remembering John's obedience throughout the ages.

Yet Elizabeth may not have witnessed the cost of her son's obedience to God's call. She may not have been alive when he was a recluse in the desert, eating locusts and wild honey, or facing the anger of the religious establishment whose hypocrisy he exposed. She may never have known of his imprisonment. We know what John's aged parents did not know, that in calling leaders to repentance and denouncing Herod's sin, their beloved son would die a martyr's death.

None of us knows what the future holds, either for ourselves or those we love. We are not in control. God does not ask for a five-year plan for discipleship or give one to us; he asks that we follow the prompting of the Holy Spirit. Obedience to the call of God is always costly. It might mean we experience misunderstanding, have doors shut in our face or suffer for refusing to follow practices that are unethical. Jesus promised his disciples that they would have 'tribulation' (John 16:33, ESV) and the same is true for us. Our response should not be to anticipate the future and take measures to protect ourselves, but to recognise the cost and, like John, to be faithful to Jesus. It is often through our obedience to God that wrong is challenged and God's will is done.

Paul's words to the Christians in Corinth are relevant today. Let's apply them to our own lives in God's service: 'Be on your guard; stand firm in the faith; be courageous; be strong. Do everything in love' (1 Corinthians 16:13–14).

ELAINE STORKEY

Who's in your past?

David was the father of Solomon, whose mother had been Uriah's wife, Solomon the father of Rehoboam, Rehoboam the father of Abijah, Abijah the father of Asa, Asa the father of Jehoshaphat. (NIV)

I wonder if, like me, you used to skip the beginning of Matthew's gospel to get to the interesting bits about the nativity. A roll-call of 14 generations with unpronounceable names is hardly an invitation into a spiritual encounter! Yet, it was crucial in Matthew's Jewish culture. Naming Jesus as the 'son of Abraham' and 'son of David' identifies him from the very beginning as the chosen one of God, the Messiah spoken of by the prophets.

The Abrahamic line affirms Jesus' Jewish roots, and having Ruth as an ancestor places him in the kingly tribe of Judah. So Jewish readers would understand the title, 'King of the Jews'. They were also aware of the covenants God made with the rulers named, and of God's promise of the Messiah. Now they would realise that the time of fulfilment had finally come.

Yet some names in the genealogy raise a few eyebrows. Judah sold his brother into slavery; several of the kings were murderers. David committed adultery with Uriah's wife and had his rival killed. Even the women aren't paragons of virtue; two were involved in prostitution. Jesus was sinless, so why name the ancestors who obviously weren't?

I think Matthew wants us to know that God didn't choose people because of their righteousness, but in spite of their sin. God uses flawed humans to fulfil his promises.

That's surely an encouragement. If we've done things we're ashamed of, God can forgive and use us. If our personal history is painful and damaged, God can release and heal us. Matthew's genealogy shows that though the past is important, it needn't have the last word. Jesus comes to bind up our wounds and restore our spirit. Whatever our genealogy, or background, God offers love and forgiveness and invites us to walk with him into freedom.

Forgiving God, thank you for my own family line, and especially those who blessed me with your truth. Help me to let go of whatever in the past might still be holding me back from fuller service in your kingdom. Amen

ELAINE STORKEY

Biblical masculinity

This is how the birth of Jesus the Messiah came about: his mother Mary was pledged to be married to Joseph, but before they came together, she was found to be pregnant through the Holy Spirit. (NIV)

Unlike our lax culture today, Joseph's culture was very strict. It must have been a disappointing shock to find that his lovely fiancée was pregnant with someone else's child. Two options seemed open to him: exposing her to public shame or divorcing her quietly (betrothal was binding like marriage). Exposure as an adulteress could have terrible consequences because women could be stoned and killed (see John 8:1–11). Divorce was kinder. It meant legally ending his commitment and sending her away, free to marry someone else.

Deciding to 'sleep on it' was obviously a good idea, because God intervened in his dream. I don't expect Joseph found the angel's explanation of the virgin birth any easier than we would today, but he went along with it. He obeyed the angel's directives, accepted Mary as his wife and they stayed celibate until the baby was born.

Matthew's story probably focuses on Joseph because he was writing for an early Jewish-Christian community where men held the authority and made the decisions. Yet the picture he gives us of Joseph stands out in sharp contrast to ideas of masculinity in most male-dominant societies. Even before Joseph understands the situation, he shows no outrage about how he has been wronged, no ego-entitlement, no display of moral superiority. He simply reacts in recognition of Mary's vulnerability.

It is an encouragement to find strong, sensitive, faithful masculinity endorsed by scripture and so evident in Joseph as a role model. When a distorted view of manliness seems to be propagated in many aspects of our culture, it's a challenge both to Christian teaching and to relationships today to get it right. It's a wonderful witness when men in our churches are motivated by care and love, and when people who are vulnerable and uneasy can find safety and peace among us.

Paul identifies the fruit of the Holy Spirit in Galatians 5:22–23. How does your church encourage its growth in both men and women?

ELAINE STORKEY

Incarnation – God as one of us

In those days Caesar Augustus issued a decree that a census should be taken of the entire Roman world… So Joseph also went up from the town of Nazareth in Galilee to Judea, to Bethlehem the town of David, because he belonged to the house and line of David. (NIV)

Luke sets the nativity in the context of Caesar Augustus, Quirinius and world history. He shows the widespread human upheaval caused by the Roman invaders' decision to tax people in occupied lands. Like others, Mary and Joseph had to trek 80 miles to Bethlehem, King David's town, where the family came from. With basic transport, difficult roads and travelling dangers, journeys could take weeks.

Yet, except for the pregnancy, Mary and Joseph's experience was nothing exceptional. Everyone was on the move. The popular stereotyping of Mary and Joseph as lonely refugees, pushed out by strangers into a stable for Mary to give birth amongst the animals, doesn't actually fit the biblical picture. Joseph would almost certainly have gone back to his family, hoping for the upper room reserved for guests. The resident family would sleep together in one ground floor room (see Jesus' parable on prayer in Luke 11) with livestock nearby, often in the same room. But with so many travellers, the guest room (mistranslated as 'inn') was already occupied so Mary had to give birth in the busy main family room. Family members would provide linen, hot water and fill the manger with straw as a handy crib.

Theologian Dick France pointed out the danger in misreading the nativity narrative in a way that distances Jesus from people's normal lives. He was born neither in a palace as a ruler, nor in a cowshed as a social problem, but to an ordinary family subject to political pressures and unjust rulers, like everyone else. This fits far better with the key message of the incarnation – that Jesus came as one of us. It also helps us pray to God in confidence and trust. When we know Jesus shared our everyday human experience and understands our needs, he brings God close to us.

Thank you, Father, for sending your Son to live life on earth and be subject to human trials. May the truth and power of the incarnation draw us ever more deeply into your love. Amen

ELAINE STORKEY

Angels do a great job

Suddenly a great company of the heavenly host appeared with the angel, praising God and saying, 'Glory to God in the highest heaven, and on earth peace to those on whom his favour rests.' (NIV)

Angelic beings are mentioned about 300 times in the Bible. In the vision of Isaiah, seraphs surround God's throne (Isaiah 6) and in Ezekiel's vision, cherubs bring God's radiance into the temple (Ezekiel 10). Angels minister to Jesus in the wilderness (Matthew 4:11) and an angel redirects Philip's evangelism (Acts 8:26). Angels have voices: they speak and sing, they bring warnings or messages of encouragement, and they appear in dreams and visions. We picture them as winged, celestial beings shining brightly to signify they come from the very presence of God. Artists often paint them with limbs, feathered wings and human faces, though the Bible gives us only sketchy ideas of what they look like. Yet people they visit recognise them as angels.

The shepherds did. A single angel first gave the terrified men the message of the Saviour's birth, followed by a whole chorus of angels praising God. The experience was so powerful that the shepherds left their sheep to seek out the baby and became eyewitnesses of the nativity. Their testimony was treasured by Mary.

Sometimes angels visit us today. When my father, aged 69, underwent an emergency operation we were told it was unlikely he would survive. I prayed by his bedside for hours, asking God for healing. When he recovered consciousness, he described being aware of an angel sitting with me, drawing him back into life. He lived on in good health into his 90s.

One carol service, I asked a stranger sitting next to me in church why he had come. He smiled and said simply, 'It's Christmas, I thought I might see an angel.' After emotional worship, I asked him, 'Did you?' 'Everywhere,' he replied. When God acts in human history, we should not be surprised to find angels rejoicing too.

Lord, open my eyes that I might see something of the spiritual reality that surrounds us and be ever more conscious of your presence. Amen

ELAINE STORKEY

Learning to wait with patience

'Sovereign Lord, as you have promised, you may now dismiss your servant in peace. For my eyes have seen your salvation, which you have prepared in the sight of all nations: a light for revelation to the Gentiles, and the glory of your people Israel.' (NIV)

Mary and Joseph went to the temple out of religious responsibility. To consecrate their baby son to God, they took the official sacrifice of two small birds. The story might have ended there had it not also been another person's day of fulfilment. Simeon, an old man in Jerusalem, had long been praying for the Messiah, and God promised him he would live to see it. The Holy Spirit prompted him to go into the temple and, after years of waiting, we can only imagine his excitement. The wonderful prophecy as he took Mary's baby into his arms was his own personal testimony to the faithfulness of God.

We find it hard in our culture to wait for anything. We have developed the technology for accessing everything in the present. Fast food outlets, contactless cards, apps on our phone, rapid computer search engines and more all bring us whatever we want, often within seconds. We expect instant gratification. So it can come as a surprise to find that waiting is still woven into the reality of our human lives. We plant and wait for spring. Women wait during pregnancy. Children wait for Christmas. Students wait for exam results. And many people wait to meet someone they hope will bring them real love and happiness. We're told that 98% of real life is spent waiting, sometimes for this very moment to end and another to come.

That's probably why a fruit of the Holy Spirit is patience. Patience enables us to be content with things as they are while we wait for how we want them to be. It keeps us on track and focuses us in prayer to accept the outcome. And if we find at the end of waiting our hopes are fulfilled, patience is transformed into joy and thankfulness.

What are you waiting for right now? How well will you cope with disappointment if the outcome is not what you long for? Ask God to keep you trusting in his love and purpose for your life. Amen

ELAINE STORKEY

Honouring the prophet Anna

There was also a prophet, Anna, the daughter of Penuel, of the tribe of Asher. She was very old; she had lived with her husband seven years after her marriage, and then was a widow until she was eighty-four… She gave thanks to God and spoke about the child to all who were looking forward to the redemption of Jerusalem.

Between the end of the Old Testament and start of the New Testament, 400 years passed, but it seems that prophets continued to speak. One of them was Anna. Luke tells her story, emphasising her age, widowhood, commitment to prayer and fasting and her spiritual alertness before God. She is also a woman, but Luke doesn't see that as abnormal. It is entirely fitting that a Spirit-filled woman should join a prophetic man in prophesying over the newborn child. Anna's spiritual discernment leads her immediately into proclamation; she tells others the good news of Jesus' identity.

I have met women like Anna. My husband's grandmother was long-since widowed, bringing up the youngest three of her eight children alone. When I joined their family, I found she prayed by name for every person in our four generations, writing to us regularly with words of love and encouragement. Her legacy continues today in the lives of her great, great grandchildren.

Throughout Christian history, women have served God faithfully in different spheres of life. They have been the bedrock of families. They have been missionaries travelling overseas with the gospel. One female doctor I know started three nurseries in Uganda, bringing in income for communities to improve health and hygiene. Two unmarried sisters were still evangelising in a care home as they neared their centenaries! Women throughout the world have served God faithfully in everyday life, doing untold acts of love.

We know about Anna through Jesus' nativity. Yet she represents millions of women: young, old, married, widowed or single who respond to God's calling and empowering, but whose stories are unwritten. Their memorial is in the lives of others.

Lord, thank you for old age, and for those who continue to serve you. Help us to create a society where greater respect and gratitude is shown to the elderly, and help us to grow a church which honours and cherishes them. Amen

ELAINE STORKEY

Led by a star – and the Holy Spirit

After Jesus was born in Bethlehem in Judea, during the time of King Herod, Magi from the east came to Jerusalem and asked, 'Where is the one who has been born king of the Jews? We saw his star when it rose and have come to worship him.' (NIV)

The arrival of the Magi in Jerusalem created quite a stir. Herod immediately took advice from his chief priests and sent them on to Bethlehem, with instructions to return. Thankfully, they didn't. But what can we learn from their story?

The Magi were willing to step into the unknown and follow their deep conviction that something monumental had happened. This is extraordinary, especially considering the great gap between their own culture and beliefs and those of the Jews. Yet they were ready to seek the truth and find the one they were led to worship, for they knew his significance. Their story shows us that the need to worship lies at the very centre of our human hearts. We learn too from their discernment. They were so convinced by a dream that they rejected Herod's assurances and undertook an arduous journey home to avoid him. In all these ways, the Magi challenge us to deepen our own faith and be ready to go where God leads.

Their story also teaches us more about God. The prophets in the Old Testament had long seen that God was not just for the Jews but also creator of the whole world. Now, God confirms this by reaching out beyond the confines of Israel so these distant people can share in the birth of his Son.

Today, as our culture drifts further away from God and evangelism is hard, we need to remember that God has access to the hearts and minds of people across the globe. Irrespective of their traditions and beliefs, people half a world away are finding Christ's salvation for themselves. The Magi's story teaches us to pray in faith that people from the ends of the earth will hear the Holy Spirit and be led to God's love.

Ask God to lay on your heart a country or region where Christians are in a minority and the gospel has not yet spread much and learn more about it. Commit yourself to pray regularly for Christian outreach there.

ELAINE STORKEY

Living with the reality of evil

When Herod realised that he had been outwitted by the Magi, he was furious, and he gave orders to kill all the boys in Bethlehem and its vicinity who were two years old and under, in accordance with the time he had learned from the Magi. (NIV)

The saddest part of the nativity story is surely the murder of innocent children. Thanks to the angel appearing to him in a dream, Joseph was warned of Herod's intentions and took Jesus and Mary to safety in Egypt. But mothers throughout the region suffered heartache from the weight of evil unleashed by Herod's anger. Both these incidents pointed back to prophecies made centuries before. No one then could have predicted that they would be fulfilled at this time and place. Matthew helps his readers understand the nature of prophecy, but nothing could diminish the pain and anguish of the bereaved parents.

Many ruthless dictators have killed their own people throughout history. Even as I write this, atrocities are happening across the globe and people who have done no wrong are being killed on the whim of the powerful. Opponents are annihilated whenever they raise their voices because weak rulers cannot allow any opposition. Herod's murder of the innocents reminds us that Jesus was born into a world of sin and brokenness, where he too would suffer injustice and hatred. We know from all the events of our day that the power of evil holds many people in its grip and many who are innocent continue to be imprisoned, tortured and killed. Satan is active. Paul reminds us that we wrestle against 'the powers of this dark world and against the spiritual forces of evil in the heavenly realms' (Ephesians 6:12).

That is why we need to hold on to the deepest message of the nativity, that Christ came as one of us, in a world marred by sin, to show us how to fight evil and to return love for hate and forgiveness for revenge. The victory over sin belongs to him. Until he comes again, he asks us to hold on to truth, persist in faith and stay vigilant in prayer.

Father God, our hearts break when we read of brutality and abuse to children and vulnerable people. Please help your church to stand against the power of evil, and to show the world the power of love. Amen

ELAINE STORKEY

The promise of Christ's return

He was taken up before their very eyes… Suddenly two men dressed in white stood beside them. 'Men of Galilee,' they said, 'why do you stand here looking into the sky? This same Jesus, who has been taken from you into heaven, will come back in the same way you have seen him go into heaven.' (NIV)

The second coming is mentioned often in the New Testament. In the Acts of the Apostles, Luke gives us the angels' assurances that Jesus will come again. Jesus talks about it himself in the gospel of Matthew, describing signs to expect. The book of Revelation gives us dramatic images of Jesus' return. Paul, James, Peter and John mention it in their letters to the churches. Just as many Old Testament prophecies about the Messiah were fulfilled by Jesus in his birth, life and death, prophecies yet unfulfilled relate to the second coming.

However, these references to the second coming show a very different Jesus from the one we know in his earthly life. We no longer see a vulnerable baby, or a preacher and healer who suffers injustice and is put to death. In the second coming, Jesus is pictured arriving in splendour and glory, accompanied by angels and the armies of heaven. It will be a public, cataclysmic event. We will see that his name is 'King of kings and Lord of lords' (Revelation 19:16). He will be the one before whom every knee will bow and every tongue confess as Lord (Philippians 2:10–11). In his second coming, Jesus will wrap up history to bring it to its conclusion, ushering in the new heavens and new earth.

The earliest Christians knew these prophecies well and their lives were lived in the expectation of Christ's return. Ours are not. With two millennia since the first coming of Christ, the second coming receives little attention in most churches. Yet it is closer now than ever before. Since biblical authors assure us it will happen, many signs in our world today suggest that we might need to take this seriously and recover some of its urgency.

Why do you think so little is preached in our churches about the second coming? What influences the way you think about it yourself?

ELAINE STORKEY

Keeping watch for Christ's return

**'If anyone says to you, "Look, here is the Messiah!" or, "There he is!"
do not believe it. For false messiahs and false prophets will appear
and perform great signs and wonders to deceive, if possible, even the
elect… Therefore keep watch, because you do not know on what day
your Lord will come.' (NIV)**

We live in an age sceptical about any predictions of a second coming. Many
cult leaders in the last century forecasted dates on which the world would
end or when Christ would return and led followers into disaster, and then
when the predicted day passed normally, they simply reported that God
had a change of heart and took credit for it!

Jesus himself warns us against gullibility, reprimanding people who
think they've worked out God's plan for the future. The message Jesus
gives is loud and clear; no one knows when he will return. That was true
even in the first century. People saw Jesus' end-time prophecies being fulfilled in the slaughter and bloodshed culminating in the fall of Jerusalem in
AD70. Yet more was to come. As the centuries have passed, wars, catastro-
phes, famines and earthquakes have all reminded us of biblical prophecies.
Even climate change and global viruses have an 'end-time feel' about them.
These signs rightly alert us, yet only God knows when Christ will return.

Jesus also warns against the opposite danger: complacency, when we
shrug our shoulders, believing it won't happen or at least, not in our lifetime. He tells parables about people living as they like, lulled into indiffer-
ence by their master's absence, then taken unawares by his return. Before
Christ comes, we need to get things in order and be ready to meet him. We
face some urgency to assess our hearts and lives and where our values lie.

Satan uses complacency to undermine our effectiveness. He doesn't
bother telling Christians that there is no God, or there is no hell. He simply
whispers that there is no hurry. Jesus urges us otherwise: to live each day
faithfully serving God, in constant watchfulness for his return.

---

*Father God, we thank you that Jesus is the King of kings and Lord of lords, and
we ask you to help us to live our lives better in readiness for his return. Amen*
ELAINE STORKEY

Enabling all ages to grow in faith

Anna Chaplaincy

Living Faith

Messy Church

Parenting for Faith

BRF is a Christian charity that resources individuals and churches. Our vision is to enable people of all ages to grow in faith and understanding of the Bible and to see more people equipped to exercise their gifts in leadership and ministry.

To find out more about our work, visit
brf.org.uk

This book engages with two great Christmas hymns: the Magnificat and Benedictus. It is also rooted in poets, prophets and the theology and devotional writing of the black theologian and mentor to Martin Luther King Jr., Howard Thurman. Using the *lectio divina* approach to passages drawn from Isaiah and Luke, *An Advent Manifesto* is an invitation to pray and practise that most ancient Advent prayer, 'Come, Lord Jesus, come.'

An Advent Manifesto
Daily readings and reflections from Isaiah to Luke
Martyn Percy
978 1 80039 094 2 £9.99
brfonline.org.uk

In 25 short reflective pieces written by Claire Musters, we travel through promise and preparation to joy, peace and finally love. Along the way we encounter a choir of 40 diverse voices sharing their favourite carols, hymns, poems and prayers, illustrated throughout with original colour artwork. This Christmas, let us take the time to slow down, reflect and thank God for all the ways he is at work in our lives each day.

Christmas Voices
Reflections, carols, poems and prayers for the festive season
Claire Musters
978 0 85746 230 4 £9.99
brfonline.org.uk

To order

Online: **brfonline.org.uk**
Telephone: +44 (0)1865 319700
Mon–Fri 9.30–17.00

Delivery times within the UK are
normally 15 working days. Prices are
correct at the time of going to press
but may change without prior notice.

Title	Price	Qty	Total
An Advent Manifesto	£9.99		
Christmas Voices	£9.99		
Day by Day with God (Sep–Dec 2023) – single copy	£4.95		
Day by Day with God (Jan–Apr 2024) – single copy	£4.95		

POSTAGE AND PACKING CHARGES			
Order value	UK	Europe	Rest of world
Under £7.00	£2.00		
£7.00–£29.99	£3.00	Available on request	Available on request
£30.00 and over	FREE		

Total value of books	
Donation	
Postage and packing	
Total for this order	

Please complete in BLOCK CAPITALS

Title .... First name/initials .... Surname.................................

Address..

.... Postcode ....

Acc. No. .... Telephone ....

Email...

Method of payment

☐ Cheque (made payable to BRF) ☐ MasterCard / Visa

Card no. ☐☐☐☐ ☐☐☐☐ ☐☐☐☐ ☐☐☐☐ ☐☐☐☐

Expires end M M Y Y Security code ☐☐☐ Last 3 digits on the reverse
of the card

Registered with
FUNDRAISING
REGULATOR

Please return this form to:
BRF, 15 The Chambers, Vineyard, Abingdon OX14 3FE | **enquiries@brf.org.uk**
For terms and cancellation information, please visit **brfonline.org.uk/terms**.

Bible Reading Fellowship (BRF) is a charity (233280) and company limited by guarantee (301324),
registered in England and Wales

Each issue of *Day by Day with God* is available from Christian bookshops everywhere. Copies may also be available through your church book agent or from the person who distributes Bible reading notes in your church.

Alternatively you may obtain *Day by Day with God* on subscription direct from the publishers. There are two kinds of subscription:

Individual subscriptions
covering 3 issues for 4 copies or less, payable in advance
(including postage & packing).

To order, please complete the details on page 144 and return with the appropriate payment to: BRF, 15 The Chambers, Vineyard, Abingdon OX14 3FE

You can also use the form on page 144 to order a gift subscription for a friend.

Group subscriptions
covering 3 issues for 5 copies or more, sent to one UK address (post free).

Please note that the annual billing period for group subscriptions runs from 1 May to 30 April.

To order, please complete the details on page 143 and return with the appropriate payment to: BRF, 15 The Chambers, Vineyard, Abingdon OX14 3FE

You will receive an invoice with the first issue of notes.

All our Bible reading notes can be ordered online by visiting
brfonline.org.uk/collections/subscriptions

Day by Day with God is also available as
an app for Android, iPhone and iPad
brfonline.org.uk/collections/apps

All subscription enquiries should be directed to:
BRF, 15 The Chambers, Vineyard, Abingdon OX14 3FE
+44 (0)1865 319700 | **enquiries@brf.org.uk**

DBDWG0323

DAY BY DAY WITH GOD GROUP SUBSCRIPTION FORM

> All our Bible reading notes can be ordered online by visiting
> **brfonline.org.uk/collections/subscriptions**

The group subscription rate for *Day by Day with God* will be £14.85 per person until April 2024.

☐ I would like to take out a group subscription for .... (quantity) copies.

☐ Please start my order with the January 2024 / May 2024 / September 2024* issue. I would like to pay annually/receive an invoice* with each edition of the notes. (*delete as appropriate)

Please do not send any money with your order. Send your order to BRF and we will send you an invoice.

Name and address of the person organising the group subscription:

Title .... First name/initials .... Surname ....

Address ....

.... Postcode ....

Telephone .... Email ....

Church ....

Name and address of the person paying the invoice if the invoice needs to be sent directly to them:

Title .... First name/initials .... Surname ....

Address ....

.... Postcode ....

Telephone .... Email ....

We will use your personal data to process this order. From time to time we may send you information about the work of BRF. Please contact us if you wish to discuss your mailing preferences **brf.org.uk/privacy**

Please return this form to:
BRF, 15 The Chambers, Vineyard, Abingdon OX14 3FE | **enquiries@brf.org.uk**
For terms and cancellation information, please visit **brfonline.org.uk/terms**.

BRF

Bible Reading Fellowship is a charity (233280) and company limited by guarantee (301324), registered in England and Wales

To order online, please visit **brfonline.org.uk/collections/subscriptions**

☐ I would like to give a gift subscription (please provide both names and addresses)
☐ I would like to take out a subscription myself (complete your name and address details only once)

Title _____ First name/initials _____ Surname _____

Address _____

_____ Postcode _____

Telephone _____ Email _____

Gift subscription name _____

Gift subscription address _____

_____ Postcode _____

Gift subscription (20 words max. or include your own gift card):

_____

_____

Please send *Day by Day with God* beginning with the January 2024 / May 2024 / September 2024 issue (*delete as appropriate*):

(please tick box)	UK	Europe	Rest of world
1-year subscription	☐ £19.05	☐ £26.55	☐ £30.45
2-year subscription	☐ £36.30	N/A	N/A

Optional donation to support the work of BRF £ _____

Total enclosed £ _____ (cheques should be made payable to 'BRF')

Please charge my MasterCard / Visa with £ _____

Card no. ☐☐☐☐ ☐☐☐☐ ☐☐☐☐ ☐☐☐☐

Expires end ☐M☐M ☐Y☐Y   Security code ☐☐☐   Last 3 digits on the reverse of the card

We will use your personal data to process this order. From time to time we may send you information about the work of BRF. Please contact us if you wish to discuss your mailing preferences **brf.org.uk/privacy**

Please return this form to:
BRF, 15 The Chambers, Vineyard, Abingdon OX14 3FE | **enquiries@brf.org.uk**
For terms and cancellation information, please visit **brfonline.org.uk/terms**.

Bible Reading Fellowship is a charity (233280) and company limited by guarantee (301324), registered in England and Wales

DBDWG0323